Help!
His Ex is a Beauty Queen

*Essential reading for anyone
who has ever struggled with
jealousy or insecurity
in their relationships*

By Susan Schöning

The Soul Lighthouse Publishers

Published by: The Soul Lighthouse in Germany, Munich

Copyright: Susan Schöning, 2011

First published: First edition 2011

Cover Art: Under license from iStockphoto

ISBN: 978-3-00-035369-7

For Franz:

For seeing in me the beauty of all I am capable of becoming.

CONTENTS

iv

TABLE OF FIGURES

Prologue

Urban Legend

I have never met her, but you might know her. She is the sister of a friend's cousin twice removed, and she lives in Cape Town. Or maybe Atlanta. It might even be London, I'm unsure now that I think of it.

She has recently met the most perfect man. Tall, good looking, with an athletic build. He runs his own business, and seems to be very well off indeed. He is charming, sincere, and they have so much to talk about, so much in common.

She thinks it is all going wonderfully, but when he calls to cancel their dinner plans this evening, she is not so sure. All he says is that he has some family business that he needs to attend to; on the phone she is understanding and kind, and tells him of course she doesn't mind, they can go out to dinner some other time, and she hopes all goes well with his family matter that evening.

But, as she puts the phone down, she admits to feeling a twinge of ... yes, doubt. Certainly disappointment. They had made reservations to try out that new restaurant in town, the one that is getting all the rave reviews.

She doesn't know what it is that makes her drive to the restaurant that night. Sixth sense maybe? Woman's Intuition?

She feels sick to her stomach when she pulls into the car park, and recognises his red BMW in front of the restaurant. Yes, it is his car; his registration definitely starts with those three letters.

In a daze she walks to the restaurant, and there he is, sitting at a romantic table for two, holding hands with the most stunning blonde girl, who looks like she is about to burst into tears. He must think so too, because he gently takes her face in his hands, and leans over to kiss her on the cheek, before putting his arm around the girl and pulling her close.

It is such an intimate scene that just watching it seems to almost paralyse her lungs. She runs back to her car, her breath coming in shuddering gasps. Family business, yeah right! He is obviously just another cheating sod.

She pauses by his car trying to catch her breath, searching in her handbag for her car keys, the word cheat reverberating in her head - and in a moment of absolute insanity, starts to scratch that word again and again on his car. On the shiny red bonnet. On the low slung roof. On each door. On his gleaming boot. Cheat. Cheat. Cheat.

The sound of her cell phone ringing brings her to her senses. She scrabbles for it, gasping in outrage as she sees his name on the caller ID. The cheating low-life! But before she can say a word, his voice is warm and loving in her ear.

"Darling, we have finished earlier than I thought. I would so love you to meet my baby sister, she's only in town for a few days. I have told her so much about you, and she can't wait to meet you. We're at that little restaurant we were going to have dinner at. Is there any way you can join us?"

Her heart leaps as she realises how silly she has been, jumping to conclusions like that. And then the realisation of what she has done to his car slams home, and she feels like an icy hand has gripped her heart. What on earth is she supposed to do now?

Of course, the legend stops there. We are left, gasping with horror at the twist in the story. Up until the point where we realise that he is not a two timing bastard after all but a really nice guy, our sympathies are with the girl. Perhaps you were silently cheering her on, saying "good for you", as she took her feelings out on his car. Perhaps you can even understand the enormity and strength of emotion that overwhelmed her when she attacked his car.

Perhaps, you too, have found yourself in a situation that maybe made you behave out of character for a few insane, crazy moments.

I know I have.

Chapter One:

A tough act to follow

My husband's ex-girlfriend is a beauty queen. Honestly, she is. Miss Junior High, Prom Queen, Home-Coming Queen. I'm not sure if she ever claimed the title of Miss California, but wouldn't be at all surprised to hear that she had. This lady is sensationally gorgeous, and just keeps getting more so as the years go by, not less. She is also an ex-model, a make-up artist and fashion guru, with the ability to make even a dustbin bag look great on her. A tough act indeed for any woman to follow.

When I met my husband, he was coming down from a three year work contract in California. He had left South Africa at the height of the country's "brain drain" in the late 90's, and worked first in Holland for a year before getting transferred to the States. It had been a period of great excitement, new experiences and enormous fun for him, and he had, as he so often said, the time of his life.

When that contract came to an end he returned briefly back to South Africa, (ostensibly to renew his passport) before getting on a plane again to head back to Europe.

That is of course, until he met me.

I was a single mom, emerging from two decades of betrayal and rejection from my first marriage, and was struggling to piece together the tattered remnants of my self-confidence and courage. My marriage had ended with so much resentment and anger, and the good times (for there must have been many of those) had become obscured and tarnished by repeated disappointments and broken promises.

I had been separated for almost 18 months, and was in the final stages of signing the divorce agreement when my 40th birthday rolled around. I wanted nothing more than to hide my head in the sand, and mope my birthday away in solitude and privacy, but my friends, (thank God for them) had other ideas.

They called it a rite of passage, a ceremony of growing up, and having convinced me that I really didn't need to do very much except show up, I sighed and let them get on with it.

They were as good as their word. One friend, Jacqui, organised a feast of curry and rice with salads of every description. Another, Rob, took charge of the deserts and drinks. My best friend, the sister of my heart, Irene, pulled out her ancient disco sound system from her misspent youth assisting her husband as a DJ, and provided the music. We decided to hold the party at my house, as my ex-husband had taken much of the furniture when he had moved out, and there were large empty rooms just begging to be filled with people, life, fun and dancing.

True to their word, I didn't have to do anything, and half way through the afternoon was pushed off to the hairdresser for a little pre-party pampering. I was looking good, and feeling good by the time 8 pm arrived – maybe this would turn out to be just what I needed to kick start my life again.

Irene arrived with her husband to run the music, with two of her friends in tow, blond muscle man, Richard, and tall, lanky, dark haired Franz. "I didn't think you'd mind," she smiled at me, as she introduced them. I remember welcoming them both; there were quite a few single women coming to the party, they were sure to have a good time. It never once occurred to me that I would enjoy getting to know them, or that I would ever end up married to one of them.

The party was a success, but what I remember most was Franz staying afterwards to help me clean up, and talking to me about his abiding passion and belief in Eastern philosophies as a way of life. I was intrigued, as I had followed an Eastern discipline and lifestyle for many years; it was not often one met someone who had similar beliefs, similar viewpoints, and common understandings.

Yet, as intrigued as I was, I needed time and space to finalise my marriage, and get the divorce finalised. I had to find a new home and settle into a new routine, create a new normal so that my children could heal and become strong again. And I needed to heal.

So when he came by the next day to ask me for coffee, I found a plausible excuse as to why I couldn't go. And again when he phoned to invite me out to dinner. And still again, when he asked if I needed help with moving into my new home.

He was persistent, but finally he got the message. I simply wasn't ready yet to start a new relationship. I needed time.

Some eight months went by, through the long African winter before we met again, courtesy of Irene, at a picnic in the Johannesburg Botanical Gardens. It was a glorious day, not too hot, and I had arranged to meet Irene and her family for a picnic to celebrate the return of Spring. Unbeknownst to me, she had also invited Franz, and once again, we hit it off straight away, swopping thoughts and experiences as we flirted and chatted and enjoyed each other.

Irene of course by this time was sitting, smug-like. "I just knew you two would be a good match!" she said. Irene's match making skills are legendary; she has an uncanny ability to put people together.

By the end of that picnic we both felt as though we had known each other for years – and this time when he asked to see me again, I agreed.

Our feelings for each grew rapidly, yet we were both very careful to take things slowly for the children. They had been through enough and neither of us wanted to delay their healing with inappropriate behaviour in front of them. It helped enormously that we were all friends with Irene. The kids soon got used to him being at barbecues or pizza evenings, or coming along to join in a game of cricket or a walk up the hill. They were fast becoming comfortable with him, and both liked him very much, enjoying his quiet ways and his thoughtful energy. His presence was reassuring after the chaos of the last couple of years. He cemented his ratings with them both when he helped to organise Georgia's birthday party, which became known as The Bash of The Year, and gained her enormous street cred at school.

Three's a Crowd

It was about this time that I realised two things. One, that I was falling for this guy, and I was really enjoying having him around. It had been over two years since my marriage had ended, and I was feeling ready to explore this new relationship. It felt right, somehow, and I wanted to take the risk and see whether this could develop into something beautiful.

The second thing that I was becoming aware of, was how big a role his ex-girlfriend still played in his life. When he had left California, they had broken up, but remained firm friends - they spoke at least three or four times a week with tons of daily emails and messages whisking back and forth between the two of them.

He told her everything. He had helped to set up her business while he was with her, and she seemed to rely on him completely still in this, and every other regard. She knew his family and was constantly in touch with them, updating her presence in their minds regularly.

I was beginning to feel increasingly uncomfortable with it all. He had had such an amazing couple of years in the states, and had clearly loved every minute of it, and he spoke of the things he had done, the experiences he had had and the fun of it all, often. And of course, she was part of all of those stories, all of those experiences.

I was torn. I wanted to hear about his life, and share in his experiences, but oh, I so didn't want to keep hearing about how good his life was with another woman. She was by all accounts, a vibrant, beautiful, fun loving, warm woman, and he found himself completely besotted and captivated by her during his time there.

I asked him, in those early days, 'why then, did you leave her behind? If it was that good, why didn't you consider staying in the States and marrying her?' I was unprepared for his answer. "Oh, we couldn't get married," he said. "She's almost 20 years older than I am. We both knew that it would only ever be a fantasy, a beautiful, glorious, temporary time for both of us."

He found it an interesting coincidence that I was in a similar field to her. I work as a Spiritual Counsellor and Energy Healer, she works as a psychic. I teach meditation and spiritual development from an Eastern perspective, she teaches western spirituality. I get asked often to give talks, run seminars, hold presentations or key note addresses, - so does she.

The more I heard about her, the more I realised that this woman was one tough act to follow, and I wasn't sure that, with my still fragile confidence and tattered self-worth, I could pull it off.

The first crisis came when he told her that he had met me, and he told her that I was divorced with two young children. Quick as a flash, she came back, warning him not get involved with me, that I was too damaged and too needy to be ready for a relationship. When he told her that he wanted to pursue a relationship and see where it went, she upped the campaign, and starting sending him all sorts of internet reports on how damaging it would be for the children, how selfish I was being as a mother, and how any good mother would wait before exploring a new relationship until her children were older.

I was furious, but didn't show it. The one thing that I had done throughout the divorce, throughout the years of recovery, and indeed even in this new relationship, was to put my children first. They hadn't yet seen Franz even hold my hand, or kiss me on the cheek. We had been very careful not to distress them in any way. I had studied traditional and spiritual psychology extensively, (amongst many other disciplines) in preparation for my work as a counsellor. I ran a busy practice dealing with exactly these kinds of issues. I taught life skills and facilitated group sessions for recovery from trauma. How dare this woman intimate that I was being a bad mother by starting a new relationship with Franz?

He laughed it off. "She's just jealous that I have met someone and that I am falling in love with you," he said. "She'll come round, she'll love you, you'll see."

I wasn't sure that I wanted her to love me, though. I actually wasn't sure that I wanted this other woman, his ex-girlfriend, to be part of our new love. But, I kept my mouth shut – after all, what guy wants to find out that the new woman he is dating has 'jealous issues'? Even just saying that word to myself made me cringe. How awful, I was behaving as though I was jealous. And so, I tried very hard to not comment, not react, when he mentioned that they'd spoken on the phone earlier, or when he would be telling me a story about a holiday they had taken in Hawaii, or their trip to Holland when he had shown her where he had used to live, or how New Year was celebrated in the States.

"Don't react, don't respond," became my mantra. "He'll stop talking about her soon enough, she can't keep this up forever."

I was wrong. When she realised that I was becoming part of his life, and that he was talking about me and the things we were beginning to do together, she upped the ante and was soon sending him loving letters and emails, little presents and cards to remind him of their beautiful times together, new photographs of her in some new pose or outfit, with provocative little messages. He found it amusing, I found it hurtful. For him it was simply an extension of the fun they had had together, continuing in a different way. For me however, it felt as though she was flaunting herself in front of me and was saying loud and clear "You'll never keep him. Look at what he had, what he can have any moment he chooses. I am more important in his life, and I'm here to stay. He was mine long before he ever met you."

In despair, I googled her. He had told me some time before that he had designed her website, and she had quite a strong presence on the internet, but I had never gone on to have a look. She was supposed to be his ex-girlfriend after all. I don't think I would have ever wanted to know much about her if she hadn't been such a present energy in his current life, but, because I was increasingly feeling that she was not really very ex after all, I wanted to know what I was up against.

My heart stopped when the image appeared on the screen. This woman was not simply beautiful, she was luminous, glorious, goddess like. She had an extensive photo library promoting herself and her services, and I sat, obsessively looking at her face, her figure, her hair, her smile. At 58, she was sensational.

I have never thought that of myself as beautiful, more like okay looking, with a pretty average figure. At 40, I already had wrinkles and lines appearing on my face. This is what he had spent 3 years of his life with. I couldn't begin to compare. At 40, I already looked older and more worn out than she did, at nearly 20 years my senior.

For an instant, I held a vision of me growing older, naturally, normally, the years beginning to show on my face and my body, and I suddenly knew that I couldn't follow this act. I couldn't age anywhere near this well. Hell, I couldn't even compare now. How would he feel when he looked at me at 50, or 53, and realised that I was not an eternal beauty like this amazing creation. If I stayed with this man, every day, every year would bring added pressure to remain young and vibrant, just to keep him interested. He would soon begin to compare me, and anyone could see, I was at a severe physical disadvantage.

Still I said nothing. I mean, how could I now? Jealousy is such an ugly word, and to admit it to ourselves, that deep down we are jealous, that we feel inferior, insecure, and inadequate, is so taboo, so frowned on, so ugly. I swallowed it down, and tried to smile it through.

In every other way, this man was wonderful. He was fantastic to my children and they were beginning to relate to him more and more as a friend. He was caring and considerate, except for this one issue, which surely was my problem, not his? I was the one who was jealous and full of comparisons. He was a beautiful lover, a stimulating and thought provoking conversationalist, a partner that I could explore my passions and interests in Eastern philosophies with. We had so many things in common. Surely I could work this one through without him ever finding out how small I was beginning to feel, how unequal I considered myself to be.

"Tell him about your past," advised Irene. "Maybe if he's hearing about your life, he'll get the hint that it's hurting you, and stop doing it." But of course, my past wasn't fascinating or fun or glorious; rather it had been painful, and so I had nothing but relief to convey to him that it was all over at last.

As these things have a way of doing, things came to a head one weekend. Little things, yet strung together became too much. He called me by her name, not once but twice, each time cutting me with ice cold daggers in my heart. He took me to a concert telling me on the way there of the concerts and wonderful events that he had attended in California. I listened miserably, feeling more and more worthless. Was there nothing I could offer this man to make him feel as much excitement or enjoyment? He took me home that night, and I asked him what he liked about being with me. His reply at the time devastated me. "I love that you are quiet and gentle and soft," he said. "You are so easy to be with, so simple and undemanding."

I didn't sleep at all that night. His talk of California was so full of new places and exciting adventures, of vibrancy, passion and fun. It was different and it enlivened him, anyone just listening to his stories of his years there could see that. All I could offer him was quiet, and gentle and simple. It was like he had branded BORING on my forehead. I flinched as I remembered my ex-husband slamming out of the door .... "I need some fun, some excitement in my life," he had flung at me as a parting shot. "Life with you is just so mind-numbingly dull, and I need more."

"You'll never keep him," whispered that goddess like beauty in my head. "You are too simple for him, you can never offer the life he craves."

She was right. I had been too dull, too boring, and too ordinary to hold my first husband; what on earth made me think that this man would want to be with me? I was too small for this man, too inadequate, too uninteresting. Best I got out of this now before my children became even more attached, before I fell in love with him any further. This would hurt, in a way that ending my marriage never had. I had allowed myself to feel for this man, to hope and dream. Stupid, stupid woman.

As if she intended to confirm my decision, I received a letter from her the very next day. How had she gotten my email address? Obviously he had given it to her. She wrote of how she wanted us to be friends, how she loved Franz deeply and that she was glad that I was in his space to love him as much as she did. I read it feeling angry, betrayed, confused. She had written me this email, that seemed to say one thing, but somehow it felt like she was really saying something else entirely. It was then that I saw she had copied it to him and his family. This letter wasn't meant for me at all. It was yet another part of her campaign to reinforce in everyone's minds how wonderful and special she was.

I couldn't play this game. I couldn't do this. Unable to face him, I emailed him and told him that it was over, as nicely as I could. I cancelled all my clients for that day, because I couldn't stop the tears; I cried my eyes out for the rest of the day.

Reconciliation

He was stunned when he read my email. "But why," he said. "I am so in love with you, everything is going so beautifully, I don't understand why?"

I told him then, how hurt and excluded I was feeling by his continued relationship with his ex. How inadequate and inferior I felt. How I went cold inside when I heard her name, how my heart raced when I realised that there was nothing I could offer him to compare with her. How small my life was compared to the life he had led in California, how I could never, ever be anything like what he had had before.

He asked what I needed from him. I told him I needed him to end it with her if I was going to be part of his life. "But she's just a friend now," he said. "I don't love her that way anymore, I love you."

"I just can't do it," I said. "I feel as if there are three of us in this relationship, and one of us needs to leave. It's unfair on both of us, really."

It was unfair. Unfair on me, because I was forcing myself to live in the impossible shadow of this ever present woman. Unfair on her, because maybe she really thought that he would return to her if she stayed in his life as a constant reminder of how simple life was now, compared to how much fun and how vibrant it had all been with her.

"Then I will end it with her," he said. "You should have told me earlier, that this was upsetting you so much. I love you and want to build a future with you. I'll tell her today."

I wish I could say that was the end of it, but of course, it wasn't. She alternated between being needy or desperate or sad, demanding his attention; and manipulative, creating all sorts of business issues that required him to speak to her. She had a knack for phoning in the evening when we were about to go into a movie, or sit down to supper, almost as if a sixth sense was guiding her to phone at the most visible time, announcing each time, "I'm still here."

It was as if she wouldn't go away, and he found himself in a space where he didn't want to hurt her, but he didn't want to lose me either

"Let it go," said Irene. "For God's sake, she's in California, on the other side of the world."

I knew that, but how could I explain that although her physical presence was 12 000 miles away, her emotional energy was haunting me. I couldn't escape, couldn't breathe, and the only way out of it was to end it with him – or have it out with her.

In the end of course, I did just that. I wrote her an email (not a very nice one, I must admit) telling her how cruel and mean I found her, how their relationship had finished some two years before and how she was affecting not just our relationship but his happiness.

I told him finally, that it was her or me. Not this "half in, half out" of two relationships. It might well work for him. It had become impossibility for me.

He chose me.

They got married and lived happily ever after, right?

Undoing The Damage

The damage of the past months had been immense. True, she was out of the picture, true, he had now blocked her email address and phone number on his computer and mobile phone, true, her name no longer came up in conversation.

The damage was within me. I now felt inadequate and ugly, boring and insufficient. I had lost whatever self-confidence I had gained since my divorce, and felt like I was back at square one. I was insecure and frightened and vulnerable - and unable to talk about it to anyone, because inevitably the response would be, 'come on, she's gone now, nothing to be jealous about!'

I nursed it inside of me. Brooded about the pressure I now felt about growing older, going through menopause, desperately trying to look younger than my age because that's what he would expect from his past experience.

I wouldn't let him take photographs of me, because I didn't want a tangible visual comparison of what he used to have and what he had settled for. I worried about whether I was good at my work, - after all, she did such a similar job to me, and I now believed that I was inferior to her in every way, which in turn created a complete crisis in my practice. I began to panic about what I looked like, worry about my face and figure as I had never worried in the past, convinced that if I didn't try hard enough he would one day realise what a drab little moth I was compared to her butterfly existence.

Her voice reverberated through my head ... "You'll never keep him, why would he want you?" ... next to his voice ... "I would go back tomorrow, it was the most fantastic time, the best three years of my life!" ... superimposed on an image of my ex-husband ... "You are so mind-numbingly dull." I couldn't shake them, couldn't get rid of them.

I kept it inside of me, not saying anything, keeping the outside me smiling and cheerful. I was a counsellor, for Heaven's sake. I helped other people to deal with these kinds of issues. I couldn't be very good at it if I couldn't even help myself.

(Forgetting of course, that it is a very bad counsellor who takes herself on as a patient). Perspective and clarity are the result of distance, emotional calmness and non-attachment, none of which I was capable of achieving in this state on my own.)

I would hold it inside, feeling brittle and fragile, until the feelings of insecurity and lack overwhelmed, and then I would explode as fear and terror absorbed me.

We had the most horrific arguments, that appalled me. Who was this person who acted so badly and said such terrible things? I had never behaved this way before.

Each time we'd sort it out. Patiently, he would help me recover, feel better, find temporary security, until the next time I felt threatened or insecure again. Until I would lose it completely all over again.

This calm, gentle, soft woman he had fallen in love with became a screaming bitch, driven to a frenzy with the constant voice inside my head telling me …"and he's mine, always will be", on the same loop as his voice saying …"she was a glorious, wonderful, temporary fantasy" next to … "boring, boring, dull"

How could I ever rate against a fantasy?

We never heard from her again. But her energy haunted our relationship, and sucked the joy out of my life. Whenever we had an outing or an experience, some part of the day would be ruined for me by this inner feeling that he'd had more fun on the other side of the world, that this was just a poor second, nothing new or unique or fantastic. Just predictable, and safe and ordinary. Dull. Boring.

Throughout our engagement and the first few years of our marriage before we moved back to his home country, Germany, I felt almost schizophrenic – loving my new man, and our new marriage, all the while trying to hide the very real scars that the start of this relationship had caused.

I was wounded, devastated, disabled by it all. And I couldn't talk about it to anyone.

Chapter Two:

The Green Eyed Monster

It took quite a while before I could admit even to myself that what I was really suffering from was jealousy. In the beginning, I hid behind the words "insecurity" and "recovering from my first marriage".

The very word jealousy is such an ugly, bitter, vicious word, evoking images of control, possessiveness, manipulation, or of pathetic, desperation and clinging. No-one wants to admit to ever feeling less than, not good enough, over-shadowed by someone else.

It was one thing to silently carry these feelings deep inside of me; it was quite another to speak the word out loud.

Jealous.

 I was jealous, plain and simple. Sickened, crippled, disabled with jealousy for what I thought the two of them had shared together, what I believed she still represented in his life, the glorious beauty of her physical appearance at nearly 20 years older than I.

Just saying the word made me feel despicable and pathetic. On top of everything else I was feeling, I now had to swallow the sour taste this word created in my mouth.

In a flurry of accountability and responsibility (as in, this is my problem, and I will sort it out), I tried everything I could think of to heal, all the time addressing my insecurity within the relationship; surely, surely, this was not jealousy? For heaven's sake, I was a rational, intelligent woman. And because I was in denial about what I was trying to heal from, the relief in each instance was temporary.

It helped for a while; the healings, the body talk, the meditations, the affirmations; but gradually, the nagging voices would remind me how inadequate and inferior I was next to her elegant beauty and I would plunge headlong, back into a deep depression.

It is funny how the Universe works. As I was battling to come to terms with this enormous emotional overload in my own life, I began to see it reflected back at me in the lives of those around me; my clients, my friends, even within my own family.

Reflections in the Mirror

One of my closest friends told me how she had become so incensed with her husband's flirty secretary, that in a fit of rage she had thrown her half-full wine glass at him. He had ducked, but the glass had shattered against the wall, sending angry shards of glass into his neck which sliced his jugular vein. A frantic emergency episode left him angry (and with a huge scar on his neck) and her emotionally depleted and shocked at the power of her rage.

"No, not because I was jealous," she hastened to reassure me. "I was just so angry with him for his blatant enjoyment of her teasing and constant sexual innuendo."

A client told me of how infuriated she had become when her partner danced with another woman at his company's annual Christmas bash. "He never dances, ever," she fumed. "He knows that I love to dance, and yet, whenever we go out, he will sit chatting with a few mates at the table, while I dance with some girlfriends."

"I was flabbergasted when one of his colleagues came over to ask him to dance, and he grabbed her hand and they disappeared onto the dance floor," she told me. "When I asked him afterwards why they had danced together, he had said something like it was good for work relations and I should just look at it as a bit of networking."

"Of course, he didn't dance with any of the other women, just this one."

She was so angry with him that a full scale argument broke out on the way home, and continued into the night. When he finally said that he was going to sleep at his brother's house, she erupted, and, pulling all his clothes out of the closet, she ripped the buttons of his shirts and the zips out of his pants with her bare hands.

"All I could think of was that he was not going to leave me, because I was convinced that he would go and sleep with the young woman he had danced with earlier that evening," she said.

It worked. With no clothes left to wear, he had no choice but to stay at home, and so he took his pillow into the lounge to sleep on the couch. In a blind fury, she yanked the curtains from the pelmets, ripping the fabric to shreds.

She showed me the bruises and cuts on her hands. "I didn't think I had that much strength in my hands; I certainly didn't think I had that much anger in me."

When I was asked her whether she had battled with jealousy in other relationships she laughed. "Oh, I'm not in slightest bit jealous," she said. "I just need to find a good anger management programme, that's all."

Suspicious Minds

I was sitting with Joe and Isle having supper one evening, when Joe excused himself and got up to go to the loo. I watched fascinated as Ilse casually picked up his cell-phone and starting scrolling through his messages.

"Just checking," she smiled when she saw the look on my face. "Always better to keep an eye on things and know what's what."

Curiously I asked friends and clients whether they did the same, and was amazed to find how many of them checked through their partner's wallets, bank statements, or cell phones in the same way as Isle does.

Susie admitted to reading her husband's email whenever she got the opportunity. He regularly travels overseas, and as she says, "He has an entire separate life that I don't know about, that I have nothing to do with. There is no place for me in his 'work' life. Who knows what he gets up to on his trips overseas? He knows that my life continues as it always does, with the kids, and their school and sport commitments, but I have no idea of who he even speaks to when he is away from home."

Belinda regularly went through her partner's briefcase and pockets. Angie would go through her husband's cell phone statements, calling numbers that she didn't recognise, checking to see who was on the other side.

Unable to Breathe

One early morning, I was stumbling into the kitchen to make some coffee before the start of the day, when the phone rang. Now when the phone rings at 8am or so, you assume it's someone who is eager to start the day. When it rings at 6.30 am, when it is still pitch black outside, and barely anyone is awake yet, you know its trouble.

It was Charlene, and she could hardly speak for the sobbing gasps that kept trembling through her voice. She had opened her husband's briefcase the night before, to look for the evening newspaper which he often read on the train ride home. When she lifted the newspaper, however, she noticed a beautifully bound book, and curiously, she picked it up and read it.

It was a poetry book, and little post-it notes had been fixed to the sides of some of the pages, with big loopy writing and little smiley faces and hearts above the i's. "Obviously a young woman's handwriting" she wailed.

"I thought of you this weekend, when I read this poem. It reminded me so much of YOU! " said one; another read "You've told me how much you love hiking in the mountains, this poem just makes your words seem so alive …", and the cherry on top for Charlene, a post-it note with a Facebook address, saying she had just posted their latest photos and he should come on line and have a look.

 Shaking with fear, anger and suspicion, she had asked her husband Kyle where he had got it from. He evaded her questions saying that it was nothing to worry about, she was getting upset about nothing, and it really wasn't important.

His evasive talk just elevated her suspicion, until she was almost hysterical, pummelling and punching him with all her power, until in self-defence he grabbed both her arms to stop her from hitting him, in the process breaking her wrist.

At the emergency room at the local hospital he explained; a young marketing assistant had been assigned to his department for the last six months, and he was playing a mentoring role to her. Nothing more, at all, he promised her.

"He admitted that they have coffee every morning before work to talk about the day's events and schedules, and then a group from the office get together for lunch most days," she sobbed. "He says she is just a young girl who seems to be slightly infatuated with her boss, and there is nothing to worry about at all."

But for Charlene, the thing that he would normally never ever read poetry is proof positive that something sinister is going on. "In fact, he switches off if ever I read something that leans vaguely in that direction. Just last month we were having dinner with friends and he was scathingly deprecating about the whole online social networking phenomena, about how it is a giant waste of time, and now here he is flirting with some little intern bimbo in his office, and going on line to have a look at her photos!"

Charlene had spent all night, working herself up to higher, and even higher levels of emotion, and now all she could think of was that she was going to end up just like her mother, with a man who cheated on her behind her back. "The whole world laughed at my mother, while my dad ran around flirting with all the young ladies, and she just acted like she never knew a thing. And here, I am in the same space, and my husband is flirting with the young girls in his office. How many people are laughing at me?"

When we met later that day, I suggested to her that there were two issues here. One, whether his relationship with the young assistant had crossed the boundaries of what was appropriate or not in a mentor / employee relationship, and two, her response coming from a deeper space of wounding from her childhood. "I am so angry with him," she said. "I am not in the slightest bit jealous or insecure, I am just so absolutely livid with him for having this relationship with a young woman outside of our marriage. Just like my damn father!"

Over the next few weeks, she found herself sitting outside his office at home time to see who he walked out with, or dropping in unexpectedly into the local restaurants in the area to see if he was lunching there with her. She remembered the Facebook address and went online, going through the young woman's profile, her pictures, looking through her lists of friends to see if her husband was there (he wasn't), and comparing her fresh faced 23 year old beauty to Charlene's slightly out of shape, recovering from the birth of her second baby, 38 year old figure. The photographs that had seemed so damning on the post-it note turned out to be nothing more than the latest product launch, and of Kyle giving a speech.

But, strong, confident Charlene became shattered, fragile Charlene overnight. "The thought of living my life like my mother did leaves me cold," she said. "But I feel right now that I have two young babies, I am not working, I am not confident anymore. I don't know how to make this better and so I don't feel like there is any decision I can make."

Even though the assistant has long moved on, things at home have deteriorated, becoming incredibly strained. "I simply no longer believe him when he tells me about his day, and I file everything away in my head, to double check and try to catch him out in a lie later on in the evening."

Kyle is bewildered and angry by his wife's assumption that he had an affair with the young marketing assistant. "It was an office work relationship, nothing more," he insists. "It was her first job, and she was simply trying to take an interest in the department and the boss. I never asked for the damn poetry booked, never even read it, but when she gave it to me to read, I said, 'yes, how interesting' and put it in my briefcase. I found it amusing that she seemed to have developed a little bit of a crush on me, and I truly thought Charlene would too."

He doesn't know what to do or say to Charlene to make things better. "I love my wife and family, but things are getting to the point where I am worried we will be beyond repair soon," he says.

Not just a woman's problem

Brian told me of how he had installed an email programme that copied his wife's emails and forwarded them to his in-box, so that he could an eye on what she got up to in her high-powered job as personal assistant to the international marketing director of an automotive firm.

Craig shared how he had followed his girlfriend after she received a few phone calls that sounded evasive and suspicious to him. When he pushed her for details, she at first evaded, and then downright refused to disclose what they had been about. He followed her downtown on a Saturday afternoon, and watched her as she drove her car into the parking lot of a swanky hotel.

"I was livid, and full of all sorts of images of what she was going to be doing in a hotel like this. I mean a hotel can only mean one thing, right?"

Wrong.

He burst into the reception bristling with outraged indignation and anger - only to discover that she was meeting with his mom and sister to plan a surprise 30th birthday bash for him.

"I felt pretty small and mean when I realised that she wasn't meeting a man … but was with my mom and sister, meeting the banqueting manager to plan a party for me."

Jake told me how his relationship with his girlfriend was being seriously jeopardised by jealousy … his. "She is gorgeous, flirty and very sexy," he says. "All the things that turn a man's head. It turned mine, and she loved the attention. Don't tell me she doesn't enjoy it when another man flirts with her."

He often checks up on her, unexpectedly arriving at her office if she calls to say she is working late or has to show a client around a show house (she is a property broker). "My mind drives me nuts otherwise," he admitted.

A common emotion

As I looked around me at my friends, colleagues, clients, even within my own family, I was becoming aware of just how many people and relationships in my little circle were suffering from the enormous strain of misunderstandings, hurt, mistrust, and doubt.

I watched as some relationships disintegrated under anger and suspicion, leaving people bleeding and gasping for breath with the sheer brutality of it all … only to fall headlong into other relationships that were practically identical to the one they had just escaped from.

Other relationships exploded into anger and then retreated in silence, covering the same ground as old arguments repeated themselves again and again, without ever resolving the critical issue.

I heard the phrase over and over, "I am not jealous or insecure, I am simply angry with him (or her), but no, I am not jealous."

And I knew that I was not alone. There were many, many people out there who are struggling with relationships. With Insecurity. And whether we like to admit or not, with Jealousy.

Chapter Three:

When the Monster Attacks

Not many of us will admit to feeling jealous or insecure. It is a socially undesirable emotion, one that we push down and hide away from the world, because to admit to feeling jealous almost feels as though we are admitting that we are second rate, less than, inferior in some way.

Jealousy remains a taboo subject because it is so belittling, so negative and self-destructive, an emotion that has the power to make us feel ugly, unimportant and invisible. It lurks in the shadows, feeding off our feelings of inadequacy and self-loathing, until it becomes a constant heavy weight that we drag around with us, everywhere we go.

It is a hidden emotion, an ignored voice, a despised quality when we recognise it in ourselves, and an embarrassing and shameful characteristic when we see it reflected in others. I believe that it is so powerfully negative and destructive, precisely because we refuse to acknowledge its presence in our lives, in our psyche, in our relationships.

It is one of the seven deadly sins, and Dante's Inferno reminds us that there is a special place in hell, reserved for the jealous and the envious. Yet for those of us who have suffered with this debilitating, crippling, disabling emotion, we know that we don't need to wait for the afterlife to burn from this 'sin'. We're already there.

From an early age we are taught that jealousy is wrong, is frowned upon. We are encouraged to trade feelings of anger for peace, insecurity and fear for trust and self-confidence, and not dwell on those feelings that are filled with lack or pain. Indeed, we are expected to push them away, to deny that they even exist. It is a taboo subject in most relationships, intimate or otherwise. No-one talks about it; certainly no-one will admit to feeling jealous. To call someone jealous is an insult the world over.

The most anyone will ever admit to feeling is maybe a twinge every now and then, perhaps a moment of inadequacy and doubt, but never, God forbid, jealousy. It is never spoken about, never admitted to, never acknowledged; we hold it inside of us like some dirty filthy secret, hoping no-one will ever find out how we truly feel.

Perhaps the most important thing of all, is that because it is a denied emotion, an ignored inner voice, we are never given coping strategies for working through it when it raises its ugly head.

We don't acknowledge the inner fears, those raging and burning emotions, but try instead to sweep them under the carpet and out of sight. We swallow them down, hide them deeper inside, obscured from the light, until it becomes hard to admit even to ourselves that we are feeling jealous and insecure.

What happens, however, when these feelings refuse to remain obediently hidden underneath the carpet where we swept them? What happens, when the pile of negative emotion, and pain and trauma grows so big, that it becomes harder and harder to turn away from?

We end up exploding as I did .... Holding it all in and swallowing it down for months, until I felt bloated and gorged on it all, only to have it all come spewing out, vomiting out of my mouth in a steam of hot, foul tasting bile. Or losing control completely, committing physical acts of outrage, like ripping all the buttons off his shirts, or scratching the word Cheat! all over the paint work on his brand new shiny car. Or we withdraw completely, and allow ourselves to become smaller and less visible, running away from the emotion completely. Or we indulge in a self-destructive manner taking our insecurity out on ourselves or our partner, and destroying the relationship, often not because of the tangible intrusion of another person, but because of our jealousy.

Anyone who has ever had a jealous attack (and I do believe that is the right word, an attack), will probably tell you that they have been told to. "For God's sake, just let it go," (as Irene told me), or "What have you got to be jealous over?" or "Get over it and move on."

Yes, but how? you reply. How do I just let go of it, when I hear its voice repeating endlessly inside my head (as in my case), or it has become an image that I see every time I close my eyes? How do I let it go when it kicks me so hard in the gut that at times I can hardly breathe, or I wake up drenched in sweat, or I am physically sick from it all? Everyone tells me that I have nothing to be jealous over, so now I am being a fool on top of it all. How do I begin to recover my sanity? How do I just let it go, so that I can move on?

It is small wonder then that we don't like to admit it to ourselves. And small wonder that we don't recover. We just become better at hiding it away.

Psychologists and counsellors will tell us that it affects every single one of us at some stage of our lives, to a greater or lesser intensity. There isn't a person on the planet, (except perhaps an enlightened saint), who has not experienced at least a moment of distress from feeling less than, not good enough, inadequate. Marriage counsellors and couples therapists report that as many as two in four relationships will have to work through strong feelings of jealousy from one partner, and out of those, 1 – 2 relationships in four will be so devastated that they buckle and disintegrate under the weight of untreated, unexpressed jealousy. Those are alarmingly high odds, so why is it still such an ignored, denied, unexplored emotion?

Because it's ugly, that's why. And to admit it to ourselves, makes us feel by extension, even uglier than we already do.

Sick with Jealousy

The English language is littered with phrases that give a deeper linguistic clue as to what is really happening when jealousy rears its ugly head.

We use phrases like 'eaten up with jealousy' to describe how this ravenous beast inside of seems to devour us, cannibalising us from the inside; 'crippled by jealousy' to illustrate how hard it is to keep focussed when an attack threatens the very stability of our relationship with ourselves and with our partner; 'insane with jealousy' to try and explain how this sick, ugly, belittling emotion affects our rational thought and makes us descend into temporary insanity and erratic behaviour.

But really the phrase should be 'sick with jealousy', because it has such a negative impact on the entire physiological, psychological and spiritual system. Mind, body, emotion, spirit; all are seriously and negatively affected by jealousy.

When in the grips of a jealous attack, people the world over report feeling physical sensations, that sometimes overwhelm for a few crazy out of control moments, and sometimes, can be sustained for an uncomfortable long period of time of up to ten minutes at a time.

We swallow it down, rigidly force ourselves under control and the attack recedes for a while, only to return with full force when the thought, image or trigger occurs again.

This constant flooding of the physical body with adrenalin keeps the system on high alert, and unable to relax and 'oh, forget about it and just let it go' as everyone instructs us to do. As the body is prepared for a fight for survival it tenses, and becomes super-sensitive to every stimulus, every image and comment, and, no matter how small or insignificant it may be, it gets related to their threat. (Which is why of course, the non-jealous partner might be talking simply about America, but the jealous partner hears that he's talking about her who lives in America, yet again).

It's almost like having a panic attack.

We already know that panic or anxiety come from situations where the suffering seems to have no potential of let up or chance of respite in the near future. Could unresolved emotions like jealousy and insecurity be the root reason that makes these situations so untenable?

Jealousy threatens to disorientate and confuse as emotion and physical responses surge out of control, escalating sometimes to a terrifying crescendo as they consume all rational thought.

Figure 1: Mind, body and emotional symptoms of jealousy

Mind, body and emotional symptoms

Racing pulse, accelerated heart beat

Cold sweat

Increased stomach acid

Stomach Cramps and/ or headaches

Adrenalin Surges creating the 'flight or fight' reflex, which when swallowed down and pushed back create feelings of being out of control and powerless

A physical rage or overwhelming anger

A feeling of absolute dread accompanied by crawling sensations on the skin and scalp

Unable to breathe, feeling as though you have just been punched in the stomach.

Heart Palpitations

Stomach upsets from diarrhoea to constipation

Vomiting, nausea, dizziness.

Visual flashbacks and phonic loops

A vacillation between the full range of emotions from Depression through to Anger, through to Anxiety

Henry and June had been married for 4 years when he came home unexpectedly early from work one afternoon.

"The minute I pulled into the drive-way, I knew something was wrong," he says. "Her car was parked in the street, and a strange car was parked in the drive-way. Somehow I knew that it wasn't a girlfriend, there was something so arrogantly male about the Range Rover sprawled on my property."

Something prompted him to enter the house as silently as he could where he discovered shoes and clothing in haphazard piles, in the lounge and dining room. "It was as if they couldn't wait, and ripped their clothes off as soon as they were through the door-way."

He found them outside making love on the pool bed. "It was obvious that this wasn't the first time, there was something too familiar about it all," was his first thought. The next instant, he was overcome by the need to vomit as the emotion burned up and out of him. "I didn't even have time to get to a toilet," he remembers wryly. "I threw up into her potted plants next to the pool. My heart was pounding like I had just run the race of my life, I couldn't breathe. It was as if someone had kicked a hole in my chest, and I couldn't get enough air in."

The relationship ended there and then, but years later, the emotion continues to haunt Henry. Now remarried, with a young daughter and another baby on the way, he says he still feels sick when he thinks of how much he trusted her, and how much of him she destroyed on that hot summer afternoon.

Even though he is happy with Marianne his new wife, whenever he has to travel out of town for business, he feels tense and stressed, checking in on her three or four times a day, and coming home at strange times, just to reassure himself that she is being faithful to him.

"I drove past the house one day and saw a strange car parked in my drive-way, and instantly broke into a cold sweat, my heart starting racing and the blood just drained from my head; to this day I don't know how I didn't pass out."

He pulled into his drive-way, haunted by the memory of what had happened last time. "I was shaking by the time I got to the front door, and could hardly get my key into the lock, I was trembling so violently. Suddenly the door opened in front of me, and there stood my brother in-law, with a big beaming smile on his face. He had come round to show his sister his new car,"

"For days afterwards I felt shocked, stressed, shaky, and unable to breathe. It was almost as though I had been concussed and was struggling to walk in a straight path." This incident convinced Henry that he needed to address his feelings of unresolved jealousy, because it was making him sick; he and Marianne sought therapy together. "She was amazing throughout it all, and her support and understanding has helped me to finally resolve the past, face those emotions head on, and to really let it go," he says.

Angela's jealous attack took an extreme twist. Brought up in a home where her father had repeated tolerated infidelities, she became violently angry when she thought that her husband of 15 years was having an affair. He was working long hours, late into the night, and was frequently distracted as the pressures of an off-shore merger demanded his constant attention. When he wasn't working on the merger, he was travelling extensively, managing the other aspects of his rapidly expanding business.

Angela was normally very practical about his busy travel schedule, until she discovered that he had started taking his very attractive secretary along on some of those trips.

In a rage, she destroyed his office – the furniture, his files, his ornaments, - only stopping when he assured her that nothing was happening and promised never to take his secretary on another business trip again. The next day however, when she called the office only to discover that they were both out of the office visiting a client, the rage once again descended, and in a wild moment of non-control, she drove his Mercedes SLK into their swimming pool.

"I remember coming to my senses on the side of the pool, dripping wet and shaking uncontrollably," she recalls. "For a moment I couldn't make out what the black shape filling the pool was; it took a few moments before I realised that I had actually put his car there myself."

Why do these emotions consume us, and overpower us, taking control of our actions, behaviours, even our physical responses to the extent that we can be physically ill with it, vomiting, unable to breathe, feeling dizzy and faint as the blood drains from our head just at the mere thought of betrayal?

How does it have the strength to turn normally rational and level headed people into violent, destructive avengers?

Behind the towering rage and anger that is unleashed, at the thought of betrayal and infidelity behind the anxiety and physical reaction stands a bewildered confused part of us saying "But I thought you were mine? I thought you loved me? I thought I was what you wanted?"

It's a primal response of self-protection that bursts up and out of us, taking us completely by surprise, because we have been taught all our lives to deny it has ever existed in the first place.

After the attack

Soon a pattern of behaviour becomes set in place. We become experts at denial, pretending that everything is wonderful and nothing untoward exists at all. We ignore those little adrenaline surges that flare up every now and then in response to a trigger, a thought or a feeling. We close our eyes to the visual flashes that our unfaithful brain insists on showing us, try to close our ears to the phonic loops of voices in our heads repeatedly deride and mock us.

Until it becomes too much, too hard to shut out and pretend that it doesn't matter any longer and we explode.

The attack itself is short lived; we throw up, we pass out, we become destructive or violent – and after that power of emotion has ripped through us and left us depleted and wrung out, we search for a way to cope with the enormity of what we are feeling.

Some people will respond to prolonged feelings of jealousy by withdrawing and becoming depressed and feeling powerless. Others get angry, becoming hyper controlling and demanding attention and details in endless arguments, while still others become anxious and clinging, needing to be reassured constantly.

Henry recognised that he was constantly anxious, constantly fearing the worst, always suspicious. "I never put it into words, but I was always checking up on her, to see if she was telling the truth. If Marianne mentioned she had been at the mall that day and had coffee with her friends, I would find a way of double checking with her friends the next time I saw them. That's why I kept driving by at strange times. I needed constant reassurance that she was being faithful to me."

Even after Angela's jealous rage had abated she was left with the most overwhelming anger. "I bullied him mercilessly, demanding endless details, dates, information, torturing myself on whether he was indeed telling me the truth, or whether he really was having an affair with his secretary" she says.

My own response to the jealousy and insecurity I was feeling, was depression. I compared myself endlessly to her, and declared myself less than, inadequate, with nothing of value to offer. I felt as though she were a giant black cloud that always obscured the warmth of the sun, and so no matter how joyful the experience had been, she somehow took the shine off the day.

It's normal to vacillate between moments of anxiety or anger, or depression, but a predominant behavioural style of self-preservation will emerge.

Figure 2: Response to prolonged feelings of jealousy

Default Response	Depression	Anger	Anxiety
Response to prolonged feelings of inadequacy or jealousy	Withdrawal, and isolation Self-Loathing and self-denial Negative and unrealistic comparisons between oneself and the 'other' partner	Competitiveness Accusations Intense Questioning Ultimatums Control - of self - of partner - of situation - of solution	Suspicious Clinging Needs constant reassurance Manipulative and over demanding Inability to focus, irrational thought process Fragile Wounded
Verbal	Avoids confrontations and denies the cause of the emotion Maintains an "It's my fault, I really don't blame you" negating self-	Tell me what you saw in her, why was she so fantastic? What do I need to do to be better, tell me I am the best, the most important to you, the most	Do you still love me, am I ok? I cannot do this on my own, who am I without you, how will I survive?

	talk	special It's your fault I feel this way so it's your responsibility to make me feel better; you have to fix it	How could you do this to me?
Debilitating Belief	I deserve to feel this way, I am not good enough, I have nothing to offer, I am less than, inferior, inadequate Blames his /herself	I have to be better than her/him in order to win You are either 100% with me in hating her/ him, or you are against me Looks for someone specific to blame	Nobody is allowed to know because they will judge me Blames the world
Behaviour	Depressed, withdrawn, moody, listless, no appetite, or over eating, no energy No joy in life, unhappy Can swing to self-destructive behaviour, like drinking or self-medication to forget In extreme	Anger, (not just at the partner, but also inappropriate anger, e.g.: towards the girl in the checkout queue). Explosions, followed by intense questioning, needs to know the details Self-sabotage and talking indiscriminately to anyone.	Inability to focus, irrational thought process Fears the worst Fragile Wounded Anxious Suspicious, checking out details, filing all details away inside a mental filing cabinet for

	cases, self-mutilation and anger directed inwards, hurting themselves, in a subconscious "I still exist because I can feel pain," versus the isolation of "I'm invisible, and it would be better if I just didn't exist"	Creates sides Sees things in black and white Sets impossibly high targets for self, that just cannot be achieved, e.g.: I will lose this extra weight in 10 days and then I will be thinner than she was, only to swing into anger, irritability, despair when not achieved	future use Insecure
What is needed to immediately soothe an attack	Stimulation Get exercising, take up kick-boxing and really move your muscles and body. If that's not possible, then go for a run or a brisk walk, throw the windows and doors wide open and fill the house with fresh air Spring clean the house, preferably to loud, pumping	Relaxation Go for a gentle slow walk in nature Sit in the garden. Have a long cool drink (not alcoholic as that will just inflame the anger even more) Take a swim, put your feet in a cool pool and just let the water soothe you Lie under the trees and just breathe gently	Rest and Routine Go for a very gentle aromatherapy massage Fill your home with soothing sounds like running water, or soft gentle music or chimes Relax in the bath Listen to a mediation CD, Try to fill the mind with other sounds

	music Get back in touch with your friends and make sure you engage with non-related people every single day	Even though you probably are too angry to feel hungry, make sure you eat at mealtimes – skipped meals results in low blood sugar, which can precipitate an anger attack	and sights Eat soft, sweet foods, and maintain your routine, make sure you gets lots of rest
What is needed for resolution and recovery	Self-worth, self-confidence, self-belief Self-acceptance and self-worth	Trust in self and the decisions they make, and the partners they chose. Recovery of self-image and self-acceptance Self-acceptance and self-worth	Inner security Self-assurance Self-trust Self-acceptance and self-worth

It's interesting to note, that when you come down to it, the only thing really that is needed to recover from jealousy and insecurity, is not explanations and understanding, not apologies and promises never to contact the threatening person ever again.

It is all about the self: self-confidence, self-worth, self-belief, self-trust, self-acceptance, self-security, and self-assurance. It's all internal work that needs to be done, a voyage of self-discovery and awareness before we can gain that most precious prize of all - self healing.

It's about the necessity of becoming self-referred and self-aware and self-respecting, in order to reach Self Realisation.

In short, it's about learning to have a relationship with ourselves first, and learning to like – and then love – who we truly are.

Dead simple really. And it is both the hardest step – and paradoxically the easiest journey -we will ever undertake.

Contaminating our World

Whether we are in the grips of an emotional attack, or in the aftermath of depression, anger or anxiety, it's not just our inner world that lurches into turmoil. It is the entire energy field we carry around with us wherever we go, in an incredibly toxic ever present cloud.

This energy reflects the turmoil, the depression, the confusion and despair that we are feeling,   and people who come into our space will instinctively feel it and respond intuitively to us. No-one wants to be around an angry, demanding, hyper-critical person who hurls insults and blame and questions incessantly in an unquenchable thirst for details; or an over anxious person who needs constant reassurance, constant stroking and protestations of love. It's understandable that people will seek to avoid an explosive confrontation, or another suspicious, tearful argument and so, ironically at the critical time when we crave more comfort, more attention, and more reassurance as proof that our jealousy is indeed unreasonable, we unknowingly push people away by the sheer force of our negative energy field.

As one husband says; " I could feel her energy from the moment I walked into the house, at the end of a long day, and I knew, I just knew that there was another long evening ahead of us as she interrogated and third degreed until she gained temporary satisfaction. But it was always a short lived respite, as inevitably something I had said would grip her, and she would launch onto a different tack of questioning. I tried, God knows I tried, but in the end I just couldn't take it anymore. I felt like I was living on egg shells, and was constantly terrified of putting a foot wrong."

Sadly this relationship didn't make it, a casualty of unresolved jealousy, and yet another statistic of no confidence and no self-worth.

Before we even say a word, our energy field announces our mood, our feelings, our inner world to everyone around us, contaminating our work space, our other relationships, our endeavours, with depression or anger or anxiety.

Until it's not just our relationships that begin to suffer immeasurable damage, but every single facet of our life.

Key points from this chapter

- ❖ Jealousy is a socially undesirable emotion, and we learn from a very early age never to admit or express our feelings of insecurity or jealousy because of how others respond to us.

- ❖ We suppress, deny, and ignore how we feel, until it bursts up and out of us in an often uncontrollable stream of words and actions.

- ❖ Unexpressed jealousy can not only make you sick, it can contaminate the energy field around you, causing immeasurable damage to ourselves and our relationships.

- ❖ We may vacillate in our coping behaviour, between anxiety, anger and depression but will default predominantly to one defining style.

- ❖ In order to recover from jealousy's crippling attack on our lives, we need to reach a place where we can find our own level of self-worth and self-acceptance.

Self Reflection

1. Do I feel jealous and insecure at the moment? In the past?

2. How does it affect me, on a physical, emotional, spiritual perspective?

3. What symptoms do I struggle with?

4. When I have a jealous attack, how does it manifest – with anger and destruction, with anxiety and physical response or with depression and withdrawal?

5. What is my long term coping behavioural response to the insecurity and jealousy I feel? Do I respond through depression, anxiety or anger?

Becoming aware of how we respond *in the moment,* and how the emotion affects our body or mind is an important start to owning and accepting that there is a problem. Recognition truly, is half the battle.

Chapter Four:

In the Shadow of the Monster

The most critical thing to realise when dealing with an emotion like jealousy or insecurity, is *that what is happening now, is practically irrelevant.*

 It's almost the cherry on top, the icing on the cake.... or perhaps, put more realistically, the straw that broke the camel's back. The real wounding, the real issue happened years before, in those early formative years of our childhood and teenager years, during those first tenuous years of adulthood. All this current experience is doing is ripping off the scabs of old scar tissue, old hurts, until all we are aware of is that pain permeates our physical, mental and emotional body.

While I was writing this chapter, I awoke from a nightmare in the middle of the night. In my dream, I had been exploring caves with a large group of people. Some were strangers, some were friends and family, others were simply people that I knew. Suddenly an impossibly tall menacing male appeared in front of me, and without the group even being aware of it, led me off to where a hidden passage was obscured behind rocks. I remember walking behind him, without questioning, blindly following him, even though I was aware of an increasing sense of dread growing in the very depths of my being. We arrived into a circular chamber, where the rest of the group had gathered to watch as I was led to a cruel cage that was suspended from the ceiling. I was pushed into this cage, realising with horror that both sides of the cage had long metal spikes that would pierce me through the moment they closed the cage door – which they did, running me through in many different places, the blood pouring from me onto the floor, as the people around watched in mute fascination.

Again and again, the cage doors were opened, and I was taken from within, and paraded around the room, only to be thrust inside once more, pierced through by the same spikes, as they cruelly opened up and widened wounds that were soon beyond hope of ever healing.

I awoke, in a cold sweat, and sat trembling on the edge of the bed, shakily drinking a glass of water – and realised that I had been shown a metaphor of what jealousy and insecurity really does to us. It *encages us, entraps us*, so that we feel we have no way of escape, but are doomed to this sentence, this dread until we die. It *isolates and separates* us from others, from the very people we feel we should be able to ask for support and help, such as our family and friends. It *pierces us, again and again, opening wide old wounds* that have begun to scab and heal over, only each time we are wounded, the damage runs deeper and deeper, until not just our physical, emotional and mental body is wounded, but our entire spiritual psyche is in despair. It *drains* us of our life's joy and happiness. It *humiliates us* and makes us feel as though we are being scrutinised, watched or worse, *judged,* - and found wanting. And it *disempowers* us, removing our personal power effectively crippling and disabling us.

But the most glaring, obvious meaning of the dream is this: *we follow, willingly,* without question, not because we want the pain, not because we are masochistic, but because the conditioning we have received in those formative years has set the mould in place.

Primary Conditioning

The Primary Family Unit

Our Parents, Our Siblings, Our Self

When I was a very young child, my mother was a fan of the great Greek songstress, Nana Maskouri. She would play her album over and over again, until I knew all the words, all the breaths she took, the harmonies and the melodies of each song on that album. To this day, when I hear the opening bars of "The White Rose of Athens", I can sing you the entire song.

It was part of my conditioning as a young child, and it is now an indelible part of my memory.

Just like the song that I can belt out at the drop of a hat, it is also in our childhood that we absorb and assimilate the shape of our emotional safety, and our understanding of the parameters of what constitutes relationship success.

This is where we are meant to learn security and safety; that we are loved and worthwhile in our primary grouping; that we are important and visible.

Sometimes however, the lesson that is learned is not one of security and safety, but of inadequacy, where our lack of desirability, our invisibility was shown to us, repeated and entrenched in our still developing belief system, our thoughts and self-talk, long before it became manifested in our jealous tantrum, or insecure behaviour of today.

We are born, helpless and dependant into a home environment that provides our primary conditioning and exposes us to how relationships work. As we watch our parents and primary care-givers react and inter-react with each other, we learn more than just language and appropriate behaviour. We absorb the nuances and subtleties of body language, facial expression, as we are exposed to the repetition of these subtle energies again and again. All of this subconscious information becomes stored within us, remaining dormant until the right trigger awakens it from within us. And just like the opening bars of that Nana Maskouri song, we recognise the opening bars of the song, and start singing, without a second thought – without a *conscious* thought. It is just the way that it is done.

How could it be otherwise? We watched it played out time and time again as a young child and teenager.

As we are cared for by our parents nurturing and love (or indeed, lack or ironically, too much of nurturing and love), we assimilate into our emotional psyche, the boundaries and parameters of how a relationship works.

Lana was born just after her mother's charming brother had been killed in a dare-devil car race. He was the blue-eyed boy of the family, loved and adored by everyone, but most especially by his sister, Lana's mother, who then sank into a deep depression which lasted for years. She was unable to perform even the most basic of caring acts for her new baby, seemingly overwhelmed by the responsibility of looking after her new daughter, and Lana was left to cry for hours before her father would come home from work and care for her. Eventually hospitalised for her depression, Lana was cared for by her father, being passed around to aunts and neighbours to be looked after when he was at work.

She grew into a silent, solemn child, ever watchful of people and their behaviour, almost fearful of being in the same room as others. When her mother recovered enough to come home to the family, Lana was almost 4 years old, self-sufficient and self-contained for her age, and her mother struggled to relate to this strange observant little girl.

When her baby sister arrived two years later, her mother lavished the love and attention she had been unable to give Lana on her new baby. "I hated my sister with my entire being," says Lana. "I had been invisible, unseen, unheard as a baby, and yet here was this new child being loved and applauded just for being there. It was a very clear message in my head at the time … you were not important, not worthy, not wanted, but your sister is."

Now years later, Lana is able to understand the emotional dynamics of that desperate time, but the energy of rejection, abandonment, of worthlessness, have scarred her, and she is unable to sustain a romantic relationship beyond a few months. "I am always the one to end it the minute I feel compared to someone or something else, or I feel insecure or rejected at some level," she says.

The role of our parents is to instil within us a sense of SELF; that all important sense of self awareness, existence, worth, validity. We have to first be recognised as living, existing, visible beings, by our primary care-givers, in order for our own concept of the SELF to develop. When this doesn't happen by the very people who are meant to love us and want us, how do we know who we are meant to be? And more, if the parent's own sense of SELF is flawed, if they do not know who they are, how can we possibly understand what and who we are?

Are we then an extension of our parent's own chaos and tragedy, of their lack of awareness of the SELF?

We learn very quickly as an infant that in order to thrive (and in some extreme cases, to survive), to mould ourselves to what our environment dictates. If food, comfort, and affection are available, then we are able to form an image as supported, sustained, sufficient, and worthwhile. However, if just one of those three ingredients is missing, our view of what we need to do in order to just simply be sustained becomes skewed, and so we end up sublimating and suppressing our visibility in order to simply survive.

Jamie's home life was chaotic. Born to alcoholic parents, his primary care-giving was erratic – from overwhelming and spoilt rotten at times, with no boundaries other than ´having fun´ to the extreme of waiting starving and cold outside the pub, while his parents had ´another quick one for the road´ . By the time he was four, he knew that the promise of the zoo and an ice-cream was nothing more than words meant to shut him up for a while. By the time he was six, he was caring for his baby brother, battling to heat up bottles and change nappies in the middle of the night, while his drunken mother slept the sleep of the dead. At nine, his mother had come to rely on him completely to run the house, do the grocery shopping, as well as to cook, clean and care for yet another baby. She kept him home from school to play mom, so that he slipped further and further behind his school peers. By the time he was 13, Jamie had learned that he was always responsible for looking after everyone else. He learned to keep secrets; because his mother kept impressing on him that it was just 'our business, darling, nothing to do with anyone else'.

Jamie made sure his kid brothers got to school and that they did their homework, so that they could make something of themselves, something he knew he himself would never achieve. His deeply engrained belief that he has taken into his adult relationships is that he has to do everything himself, in order for the relationship to succeed. He is unable to receive love unless he has ´worked hard enough to warrant it´.

Our secondary conditioning

Our school years, teachers and peer groups

Our Friends, Community and Social Groups, School

In case you think that I am taking the blame and laying it all at our parent's feet, let me hasten to dispel that notion. All our parents do, is help to prepare the soil. It is our secondary conditioning that in so many ways reinforces and cements the beginnings of our belief system into cold, concrete fact.

For most of us, our primary family is the family unit of mother, father, sibling, (or two) and our self. With the fragmenting of the family unit in recent decades, important family members like aunts or uncles, grandparents, cousins, often live at a distance away from us, and are seen only a few times a year – only if we're lucky, that is.

Our secondary conditioning kicks in for most of us when we start school, or these days, even younger, when we start kindergarten or day care, where we realise that other people, other groups also have thoughts and opinions on what is right.

It is here for the first time, that we are exposed to emotional minefields of peer pressure; of fitting in, conformity, being accepted, or much worse, completely rejected from the group. Here, our behaviour is examined, pulled apart, accepted, criticised or approved of, and we change the shape of who we are and how we feel, behave, react and speak, in order to fit in and be accepted by this oh-so-powerful group, in the process of 'socialisation'. It is here that we are meant to learn how to work together within a social setting, and discover our place in the pecking order.

During this phase of social conditioning, we assimilate our culture's belief system and values, and learn very quickly what emotions are right and approved of (like compassion and sharing), what emotions are frowned on and punished publicly and humiliatingly (like selfishness and jealousy). In short, we learn what emotions and behaviours are acceptable and more importantly, desirable. Sharing our sweeties will bring us approval from the group and the adults around us, whereas taking a toy away from another child because we want to play with it will earn us disapproval and punishment at some level.

Within a short period of time, we become adept at pushing down the undesirable emotion and hiding it away, because the punishment is swift and cruel, not just from the adults we encounter, but more so from the children in our peer group, who are also learning the same lessons. Their response and attitude to us is a far more powerful barometer of our acceptability and policer of our behaviours and beliefs, than the adults who try to instil these values and beliefs in the first place.

For Angie, the power of her secondary conditioning shaped how she felt about herself far more than her primary group had, in terms of what was an acceptable image or what was considered pretty and desirable. They became the benchmark of what was required for social inclusion.

"As a young child I had 'lazy eye syndrome' a condition where one eye 'wanders' toward the outside of the eye," she recalls. "The effect is often disconcerting; as people are unsure what or who the lazy eye is actually looking at. Sometimes it appears that my eyes are focussed on two very different focal points altogether. It has happened occasionally (normally when I am really tired or very upset), as an adult, where I will be looking at someone and talking to them, and realise that they are unaware or unsure of who I'm actually speaking to. I have learnt to say the person's name very specifically when I talk to them, if there are more than three people in the group, to avoid the embarrassed pause that inevitably arises if my eyes are a little bit 'squint'.

"Children, though, are very cruel of another's physical imperfections, and would tease and make fun of me. I would respond by never looking anyone in the eye, so they couldn't see how bad my eyes really were. I would spend break times hiding away by myself, wrapped up in a book, because it was easier to just pretend that nobody was around than to face their teasing.

"But of course, because I didn't try to be part of the group, because I excluded myself (before they could exclude me) when it came to games and choosing teams, I was always the last to be chosen. Not just because I had bad eyes, and so obviously couldn't catch the ball (to this day, I still cannot play tennis, I just can't see the ball!), but because I had 'looked' at myself through their eyes, and judging myself lacking, held myself back.

"Nobody in my family ever laughed at me or teased me during those long years of eye exercises, countless operations, walking around with plasters over my good eye as they tried to force my lazy eye to work. At the same time, however, there was chaos within the family structure, as my parent's marriage disintegrated and the children split up – my sister to live with my father, and I to remain with my mom. They were unable to support this child being forced to confront her physical acceptance on the school playground.

The disintegration of Angie's family at the same time meant that there was nobody really for her to discuss such 'trivial issues' with.

"There were far more important things to worry about than whether I had received an invitation to the party that weekend.

"For years, I dealt with social settings and situations much the way I had when I was a kid in primary school – by wrapping myself up in a book and not meeting anyone's gaze for too long, because I couldn't face the embarrassed pause or 'who are you looking at actually?'

"I do the same in relationships now, I'm sure. I duck away, and hold back, unable to meet anyone's gaze for long, without worrying if my eyes are straight or if they actually want to speak to me in the first place. I took a degree in physiotherapy because I didn't have to look at someone when I was talking to them, it was fine for me to talk to their back or legs or whichever part of their body I was working on."

In that wonderful movie, Pay it Forward, with Helen Hunt, there is that bitter-sweet almost romantic moment where her son's teacher struggles to allow himself to relax enough to open up and kiss her. He doesn't though, because he is so conscious of scars that he received as a child where his body was badly burned and disfigured, and he is terrified that if she sees what he really looks like, she will reject him.

"I can't reject you," Helen's character screams at him, in complete frustration after he has pulled away from her yet again. "You are far too quick for me. You reject yourself before I even get a chance."

That line has stuck with me, because of the enormous truth it conveys. During our secondary conditioning, we suddenly have the opportunity to see ourselves as others see us - not our families, but the 'others' out there., Depending on their response and acceptance of us, we judge ourselves more harshly than they ever could - and then reject *ourselves* and hold ourselves back and hide ourselves in the shadows.

Danielle started school with friends from kindergarten, and soon the little group of girls were inseparable, planning sleep overs and swimming dates, pony rides and tea parties. The friendship was fine, until round about the third grade, when her teachers and parents realised that Danielle was struggling to keep up in class, her reading was very slow, and her numerical ability was way below the class standard. Her marks were getting worse and worse, and while the other three little girls were all confident, smart A grade students, Danielle was flunking nearly every test. They soon started to tease her, and calling attention to their full marks compared with her really low grades, escalating the teasing after she had scored a Zero on a foreign language test. Other children on the playground soon picked up that Danielle was the target, and in that way of children (if we're bullying someone else, then it's not directed at me) soon everyone at school was calling her 'stupid, dumbo and thickhead.' Confused and hurt, betrayed by the three best friends that she had been with since kindergarten, and realising that she was different to other children, Danielle thought she was too stupid to learn. She developed a series of alarming physical complaints, and nearly ended up having her appendix removed when doctors thought that her intense cramping and nausea was the result of a ruptured appendix. It was then that an astute doctor realised that this little girl was emotionally traumatised and mentally distressed to the point that it was making her ill, and he referred her for psychological counselling. After intensive tests it was discovered that she was border line dyslexic, and struggled to recognise the letters, words and numbers written on the board and in her text books, and that this was why she was experiencing such learning difficulties.

The damage of her third grade year, however, had been immense. Her reputation had been set, her school peers had no clue what a learning disability was in the first place, (and were certainly too young to realise how hurtful they were being to her), and they continued to call her stupid, ostracise her from the group, and make her life miserable, even though she was moved to a remedial class.

Years later, now able to read and write proficiently, and the manager of an Animal Shelter, Danielle remains aloof and apart from others, not interacting in any social group, but staying on the fringes. Her life changed from that moment on, says her mother, from a happy, joyful, spontaneous little girl who loved to play with others and be involved in group activities, to a loner, who avoided any type of team sports, or group gathering. She has never had a close friend ever, since then. She is now 28, 20 years after that awful experience.

Her secondary conditioning taught her that she was less than, inadequate, stupid, inferior. Danielle has never allowed herself to become intimate with another person, male or female, terrified that if she lets them get too close, they will realise how stupid and inferior she really is. She continues to judge herself through the eyes of her 8 year old peers, and finds herself, terribly, awfully, painfully lacking.

The final cement

High School, University/College, First Love, The ever-present Media

From the lessons and understandings (conscious, subconscious and unconscious) of our primary conditioning within the family unit, to the reinforcing structure and messages of our secondary unit of what constitutes acceptable behaviour, image, thoughts, beliefs, we lurch into the final cementing phase of what becomes our lifelong emotional blue-print ... high school, university or college, and our First Love.

At this stage of our lives, as young adults, we are beginning to examine our experiences, our beliefs, our values and opinions in the context of what we have learnt throughout our lives. We start to ask questions, like: *"Who am I really?"* and *"What do I believe to be true?"* We judge the validity of our burgeoning identity against the approval and solidness of our primary and secondary conditioning, and use that as a backdrop for the assessment and acceptance of our new identity by this new group of peers.

At this stage, as we shed restricting thoughts and rebel against parental rules and norms, we think that we are claiming an original identity, but one which in truth conforms to the group mind yet again.

Girls who used to giggle together as they went off in groups to the ice rink, are now consciously assessing their physical status in the context of their friends, the media images they are bombarded with, and even more confusing, the changed attention of the opposite sex, as hormones add spice to an already complex equation.

The teenager who refuses to listen to the sedate musical radio station that her parents have listened to all her life, now blasts the house with her heavy metal CD's ,(torture!), claiming uniqueness of thought and identity ... along with every other teenager on the block. (Or so it seems in my previously quiet suburb in Munich, which is now home to a couple of teenagers all the same age!)

As she dyes her hair, paints her nails black and rips her jeans to break out of conformity, she is ironically unaware of donning yet another uniform of conformity, that of her new peer group.

The impact of this stage is not to be under-estimated. As they struggle to understand who they are, and what their purpose of life is, as they challenge (and sometimes shed) old beliefs and identities, they are cementing the blueprint of their personality, shaping not just the person they will become as they enter adult-hood, but also their responses, actions and behaviours.

What mother hasn't watched her teenage daughter with a mixture of dread and empathy, understanding, remembering the chaos and confusion of this time only too well? What father hasn't wanted to encourage his son to 'hang in there, it will get better and easier in a few years' time'?

Sharon remembers her teen years in a cringe of agony and embarrassment. "I wasn't particularly pretty as a teenager, and went through a gawky stage quite late compared to the other girls in my class. While they were all developed with hips and pert breasts, at 15 I was still flat-chested and a podgy tummy. Of course the boys at school had no time for a girl who could iron shirts on her chest, and so when the party invites were handed out, I was never invited. I somehow became invisible, and unseen. I would feel overlooked and hated the pitying way the other girls would look at me. I was invited to my high school reunion last year, and I didn't go. I was convinced that no-one would even recognise me, or remember that I was even in the same class."

Kerry's memories of her high school years are more rose-tinted. "Looking back it seemed ideal," she said. "I was told what to do, when to do it, and even how to do it, my day was managed and constructed for me by my parents, my teachers, the society. It was all so much easier, having someone else take charge and the responsibility of the day to day life".

"All I had to do was show up in class or at the supper table, show some interest in what was happening around me and do what was outlined for me to do."

Our peer group at high school and university remind us and shape our emerging identity into what is acceptable, what is desirable, what is right and wrong. As we join different clubs and associations at University or college, we are trying on different guises to see how well they fit. A friend of mine, Michaela, spent her first year in University exploring the different religious clubs and associations available on campus. She had been brought up in an ultra-conservative Christian household, where church attendance was mandated. When she arrived on campus for orientation week and realised she could attend a Zen Buddhist retreat, or go chanting with the Hare Krishnas or visit synagogues with Jews for Jesus, she dived into it all head first. It was a fascinating, absorbing, stimulating year, and one that prompted her to change her study from psychology to comparative religions. "My parents were convinced I had joined a cult when I went chanting through the streets of Johannesburg with the Hare Krishnas and handed out flowers to strangers. I found the entire event completely freeing, and one that enabled me to finally see the God they had been trying to ram down my throats, albeit differently from the way they wanted me to see Him," she says now of the experience.

Not to be underestimated, one of the biggest influencers of our self-image comes from the constant messages blasted forth by the media. All day long, on the radio, on TV, in magazines, on billboards and posters, on visual streaming in the subway stations, the message of "...look better, feel younger, dress sexier, attract more..." The constant message screams out, targeting younger and ever younger girls with its 'image is everything' voice.

As young girls who are trying to form their own self-belief of what constitutes pretty or beautiful, they are bombarded with impossible images of beauty, that have been air-brushed, photo-shopped, artist altered, professionally made-up and hair styled into an unachievable, unattainable perfection. This is what they compare themselves to, and judge themselves against, a glossy image that has no possible semblance with reality.

A girl who has been brought up with a realistic and healthy attitude and awareness of her health, her body, her image will be less affected by the media images than one who has felt excluded, not pretty, overweight or marginalised in some way by her looks as she was growing up.

First Love

And so, we emerge from the chrysalis of our primary and secondary conditioning phases, cemented in place by our high school and college years, only to then have the mould of who we are fired in the oven of our first love. This encounter which should be sweet, innocent, beautiful has the power to shape the ideal of what our future love relationships should be.

We remember the name and the headiness of our first love, even though other people we have dated over the years between then and now may fade into a vague recollection of half forgotten (intentionally forgotten in some instances!) memories.

Most of us still hold a soft spot for the first person who claimed our heart, even twenty, thirty years later, which is just as it should be.

Alec remembers his first love with bitter sweet affection. "I had just left school when I met her, she was still in the 10th grade. I thought she was gorgeous and beautiful; she thought I was dashing and mature and oh-so-desirable because I was working which meant I had my own car and money to take her out. Her parents unfortunately thought that I was too old for her, and so they forbade her from seeing me again, which at the time, devastated me. But now that I have a 16 year old daughter, I completely understand why they didn't want her dating a guy of nearly 20 years old."

For Nikki though, her first love was anything but a good memory. "He was the school heart throb, and I couldn't believe it when he asked me to go to the rugby dance with him one weekend. He had hardly spoken to me at all before that, and I couldn't believe he had actually noticed me." What should have been a wonderful first dance experience degenerated into a nightmare when he got drunk, and then dragged her behind the rugby pavilion and forced himself on her.

"I never told anyone about that night," she said, "I was never popular in the first place, one of the invisible people at school. I never thought that anyone would ever believe me, he was the school heart throb, hero of the rugby team."

That encounter made her suspicious and paranoid of anyone's attentions towards her after that, sexual or otherwise. "It took years before I finally sought help and allowed myself to heal the emotions from that night. Years in which I was branded as frigid and aloof or judgemental and controlling. I couldn't bear to be around anyone who was drinking and would become scathing and vicious if the man I was with drank as much as one beer, because in my mind that had become synonymous with what I finally accepted in my mind was nothing less than rape."

Sandra's memory of first love is just as cynical as Nikki's. "I was fat as a child, and an overweight teenager, the antithesis of the long limbed beauty who looks down on us from the billboard advertisement. I knew that boys wouldn't ask me out unless I gave them an incentive, and I realised early on that the only thing I could offer a hormonally challenged teenage boy was sex. I was invited to all the parties, because they knew that 'Sandy was Randy', and I would allow any boy to do practically anything to me. Even the guys who were going steady with a girl would want to be with me, every weekend. "

Today in her thirties, slimmed down and vitally attractive, Sandra has not only an exceptionally low opinion of men (they will do anything for sex, there isn't a faithful man on the planet), but a crippling image of her own self-worth. "The only way I could get a man to look at me is to offer him sex"

She has had a string of relationships with married men, but has never had a monogamous relationship in her life. Each time she has an affair, she becomes incredibly jealous of each of her lover's wives and families, while at the same time protesting that she never wants to be a wife. "What's the point", she says. "There isn't a faithful man on the planet; they would all sell their own grandmother for the chance of sex."

The Emotional Blue Print

The building blocks of our childhood and teen experiences set our emotional blue-print in place.

Figure 3: Building Blocks of our Emotional Blue Print

Building Block 1	Based on our experiences as a young child with our family, our primary care giving unit
Building Block 2	Reinforced by our peers and lessons of our secondary conditioning as supported by our school teachers and friends, our friend's parents, the groups and sports we attend
Building Block 3	Cemented in place by our all-important exposures, experiences and understandings of our high school and teen years

The result is a deeply rooted, yet subconscious belief system that is formed on what constitutes the basis our relationships as we move forward into the future.

If our parenting has been healthy, and we were blessed by supportive friendships and school going experiences; if we were surrounded by positive structures as we were forming our own identity and image of who we are becoming and what our values are; then our self-belief, self-worth, self-confidence in turn, those components of the SELF is healthy, and we become well adapted, secure adults, ready for our lives in the big wide world, attracting strong, positive relationships, love and otherwise to us.

If on the other hand, our parenting has conveyed lack, and our basic primary needs were not met because of our parent's chaos in their own lives; if our secondary conditioning with our school careers and our early friendship reinforced this lack and undesirability; if our challenge of our identity and image was met with resistance and negativity; then we emerge into the adult world with a lower self-image, a skewed opinion of self-confidence and self-worth, where the SELF almost doesn't seem to exist, and what is required to create and sustain a healthy love relationship where we both feel nurtured, support and secure.

Without even realising it, we have absorbed the words of the song, so that whenever the opening bars start to play, we unconsciously begin to sway to that silent tune and faithfully repeat our programming.

Key points from this chapter

❖ Our emotional blueprint is set in place by our experiences in the primary family unit, and then reinforced by our secondary conditioning and our experiences as we leave high school and head off for university of college.

❖ It becomes like an ingrained pattern, programmed into us, just like a well-remembered tune, one that we subconsciously and automatically provide the words and melody to even though we may have only heard the opening bars of the song.

❖ The core of our emotional behaviour of today is rooted in our past experiences and programming of our childhood years.

Self Reflection

1. Objectively and honestly, if I allow myself to look at my key life experiences from my infancy up to my early adult hood, what was my primary and secondary conditioning like?

2. If I had to draw a time line of my life, with my positive experiences above the line (for they are just as powerful in shaping our programmed belief), and my negative experiences beneath the line, what it would look like?

Chapter Five:

Into the Monster's Lair

And so, the conditioning of our growing up years leaves us with either a sense of inner security and stability, or an awareness of inferiority and non-acceptance.

If we have felt loved, supported and validated at each stage of our development, chances are that we have grown into a stable, secure adult, with a concrete sense of self-worth and self-acceptance.

But what if our infancy and childhood, unwittingly and without intent, was inadequate and lacking in any way? Could this wound and scar the developing child, delivering not powerful messages of self-worth, but negative emotions of inadequacy and inner doubt?

We are all born, helpless and fragile, into a family structure that teaches us the most basic of life necessities. We absorb our environment with every breath that we take, deciphering vital clues that tell us whether we can trust that we will be cared for and looked after, and therefore we are safe and supported, or conversely, harsh and angry.

Alongside the obvious primary learnings of how to eat, dress ourselves, tie our shoe laces, we also absorb our family's belief structures, morals and behaviours, and model our behaviour accordingly.

Even as we are learning how to speak, we are absorbing the nuances and subtleties of our parent's communications styles, both verbal and non-verbal. Even as we are learning how to walk, we watch how those in our immediate surroundings act and behave and respond - and subconsciously and unconsciously we make decisions on how we are expected to walk on this journey of life.

Figure 4:　Stages of Development and Affirmation/Wounding Scale

| **Infancy** | As an infant, we are little more than a passive receiver, and have to rely on others to meet our most basic of needs, like comfort, food, clean, dry nappies, as well as for the needs of nurturing, loving and touching.

A baby who is held and cuddled and nurtured, who is fed when hungry, whose primary caregivers are tactile and verbal and gentle, develops an early sense of trust and safety, as his needs are always met, versus the baby who is neglected or ignored, left to cry, or not fed regularly, or even left passively on his own without interaction and stimulation.

The risk is that the infant then develops a mistrust that his most basic needs will not be met, learning after a while that there isn't any point in crying anymore because nobody responds to me anyway. | **The Negative Wounding** that occurs if this early nurturing is deficient in some way, is the belief that the world is a hostile place and I am not safe here. I cannot trust anyone. Nobody holds onto me and affirms my existence. I am invisible.

On the other hand, **the Positive Affirmation** that emerges if this stage is successful and nurturing is that I am loved and protected and safe. It is safe to trust. |
| **Toddler:** | Any parent of a toddler can describe the battle of wills that takes place, as the young child realises that he can do things for himself. As he learns new skills and becomes proficient at activities that previously he had to | **Negative Wounding:** I can't do this right, I can't look after these basic skills, I doubt myself, |

	rely on mom or dad for, he becomes independent and starts to explore his parameters, to see how capable he is. All parents remember the shouts of "Me do it" when we are trying to dress a child in a hurry, or the defiant "No!" as he discovers that what he wants is different to what mom wants. There is a reason it's called the 'terrible twos'! It's a vital stage of discovery and learned independence, where achievement of the simplest tasks, like dressing himself, or going to the toilet alone, or feeding himself create the basis for independent action. The job of the parent is to allow the developing child to explore his world with safety, encouraging him to try new tasks and activities when he indicates that he is ready, and to applaud, encourage and support each new milestone. This allows the child to form a strong sense of his own ability to act with intention. The child who is always discouraged or prevented or even shouted at, for touching, exploring, expressing himself, making mistakes and learning as he interacts with his family and environment becomes less sure of himself to act capably and independently.	and I need to depend on someone who can look after me. **Positive Affirmation:** My attempts to learn new skills and become independent are supported with love, in a safe environment. I can do it myself!
Pre-school:	As our young toddler goes off to pre-school, where mom and dad are no longer the primary	**Negative Wounding:** My games and

	influencers or caregivers, he is introduced to a whole new world of other children his own age and their parents, his teachers, all of whom expose him to a different approach to life. Our little boy starts to role model social roles that he is exposed to, as he tries to identify with the new influencers that come into his path. He can be a fire-man, superman and your new Labrador puppy all in the same day, and play each role with equal enthusiasm, demanding that he also wants to eat on the floor like the new puppy as he immerses himself fully into the role. He learns to initiate games, imagination, actions, which if supported by his new peers and teachers, mean that he is a good boy, or if unsupported, that he is bad. Social policing begins to make its appearance here, as we learn at this very early age which emotions are socially desirable, which actions or behaviour are non-desirable.	behaviours and identities are bad, because no-one wants to play with me when I behave this way. I am bad and maybe the way I feel is bad. I need to hide part of who I am away from people, in order to be liked. **Positive Affirmation:** I can be anything, I can explore and have fun with my friends, and learn from my teachers. I am a good boy.
Primary School:	Off to school, with its focus on learning new skills, new knowledge, new competencies, and then applying this core knowledge to achieve, across a wide spectrum of academic, sporting and team oriented activities. It is here that the self-esteem is cemented or shattered, in front of our peers and teachers, as they	**Negative Wounding:** I can't do the lessons as well as all my friends, I am not as smart as they are, I don't get good marks, I can't run as fast or swim as well, I am not

	recognise and reflect back to us our success and competence or inadequacy and lack of competence. In the lingo of the school yard, competence becomes equated with success and acceptance, whereas lack of competence means that I am inadequate and therefore, part of me is unacceptable the way I am. The child who is a great swimmer discovers that he is in demand at all the school gala's, and that the children all scream his name at sports events, as he beats the competition time and again…. Versus the little girl who tries out for the netball team and gets dismissed after only 5 minutes on the court, by an overworked teacher who has just been lumbered with the task of managing this year's netball programme on top of everything else she has to do this term. As the little girl walks off the netball court, she silently absorbs the unspoken message … I am not good enough … and makes a decision there and then never to try out for another netball team again.	as good as they are. I am inadequate and inferior, I am worth less than others. **Positive Affirmation:** My new skills are teaching me more each day, and I see the recognition and approval of what I can do in the classroom and on the sports field reflected back at me by my teachers and my peers. I am successful.
High School:	As teenagers hurtle in the confusing years of adolescence, they are faced with crises of identity, morals, beliefs and choices. They may try on many different roles and identities, picking up and discarding causes	**Negative Wounding:** I don't fit in, I don't belong, I am not good enough, I don't measure up,

	and ideals, as they seek out alternative roles and identities that will help them clarify who they are becoming as they grow towards adulthood. At this level they begin to assess their physical status alongside their friends and media models, in conjunctions with attention from the opposite sex, and form opinions on their desirability as a person, a friend and a partner. As they flirt, and dress up, as they are drawn to one group or another, as they explore different causes and social beliefs, they are really asking "Do I fit in? Do I belong?" These questions that revolve around the identities they try out, as they skirt around the much bigger questions of "Who am I really?"	versus the role confusion of I don't know who I am or where I am going, I have no direction, what is my ambition? **Positive Affirmation:** I belong, I am welcomed, I have a strong set of friendships and relationships in and out of school in a variety of different communities, I am beginning to understand who I am and what I believe.
Young Adulthood:	As a young adult, based on the positive and negative feeders of our past experiences, we then make decisions about our love relationships. Will I be with a partner, will I share intimacy and love, and have a satisfying love relationship, or am I unworthy or afraid of love, and so choose (subconsciously) a life of isolation and aloneness, because it's safer? Based on the belief system that we have internalised, our emotional blue print, we begin to unconsciously act out our	**Negative Wounding:** Nobody would want to share their life with me, I am undesirable and unattractive, if someone does hook up with me it's only a matter of time before they realise they made a

programming in our relationships.

The feeling of being lovable and worthwhile and secure in my ability to love, and in my worthiness to receive love is obviously a far healthier recipe for relationship success than feeling insecure in the relationship because deep down, I believe I am not as desirable, not as beautiful, not as worthy for love as someone else.

Our view and acceptance of who we are programmed by our experiences throughout life, colour and shape our formative relationships as we move forward on the adult journey ....and ironically, most of us remain completely unaware of the power it holds to provide happiness, or deliver continuing stress and pain.

mistake. What is love anyway, but control and lack?

Positive Affirmation: I have a lot of love to give, and am secure in my sense of SELF. I am a worthwhile mate.

The negative woundings or the positive affirmations we receive in each of these stages teach us very effectively how the world of interpersonal relationships work, and what they give to us, or take away from us. A baby who grew up in a neglected household, who struggled at school, who experienced role identity and confusion as an adolescent and was hurt or teased by his peers, is going to have a far more mistrustful view of love relationships than someone who was born in a comfortably secure home, with mature, nurturing adults, who had the time to help her through her school work, and who was secure in her role within the communities she inhabited.

Our inner security scale as we emerge into adulthood would then look something like this:

Figure 5 and 5.1: Effect of Primary and Secondary Development in terms of the Affirmation/Wounding Scale

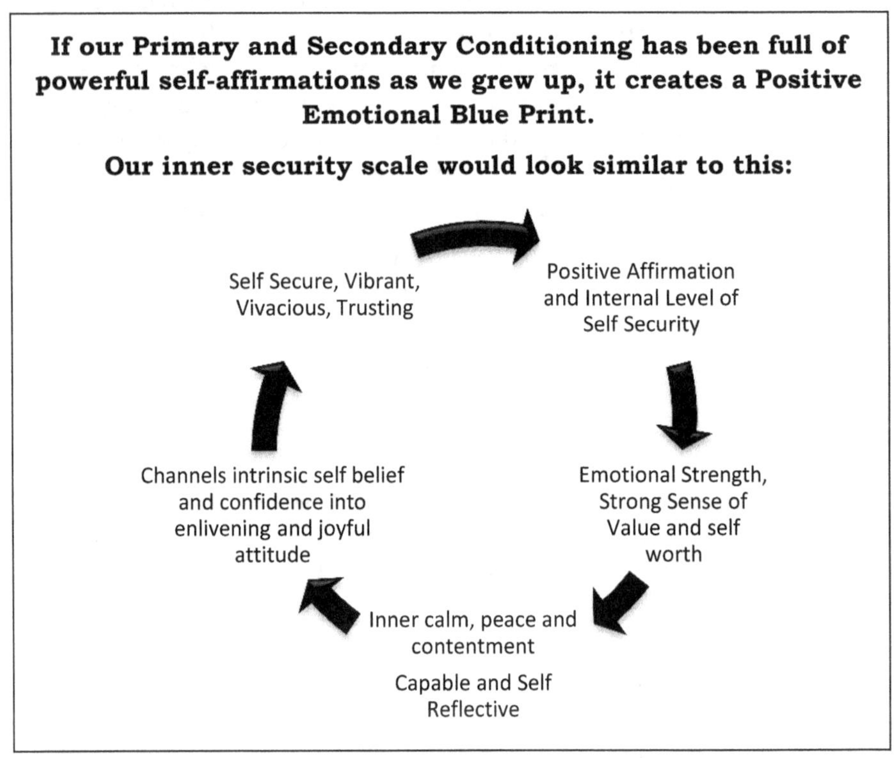

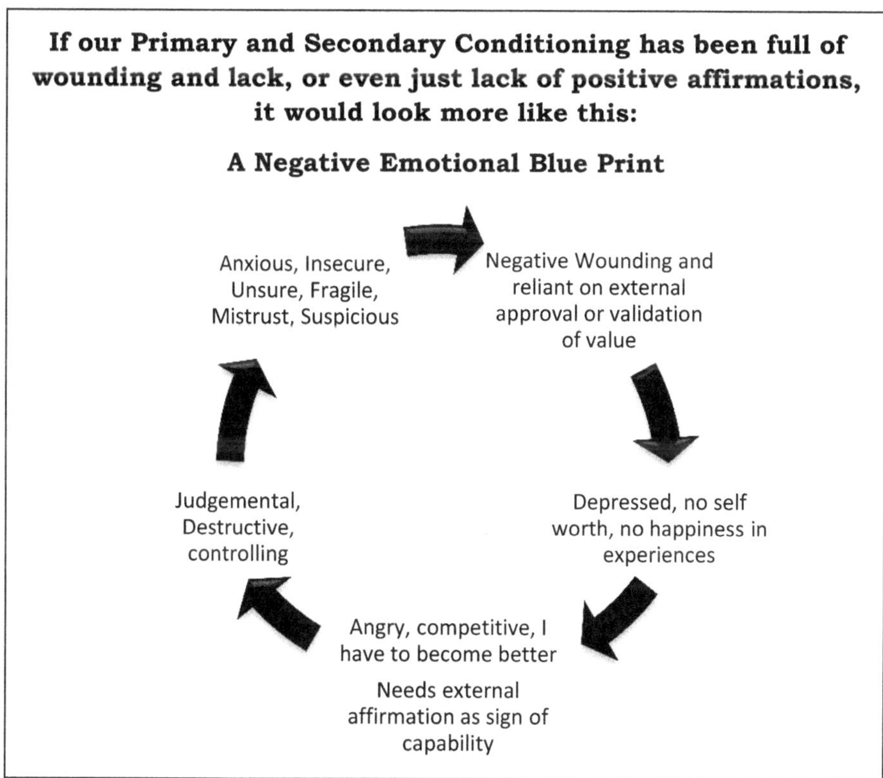

What Lies Beneath

These old wounds, old mistrusts, old beliefs that persist can lie dormant sometimes for years, until we enter into a relationship that pushes the same triggers of our wounding, so many years before.

Anna grew up watching her charmingly handsome and fun loving father flirt with all the neighbourhood wives, and the mothers of her school friends. "I used to wonder why my mother never had any friends who she would visit for coffee or who would come round to the house, like other mothers did," she recalls. "I remember going to a school function, and watching my father flirting with all the mothers who were serving coffee and cake at the refreshment table; he was a very tactile man, and was forever hugging them, playing with their hair, or rubbing their arm or back and of course, most of the women loved the attention, giggling and flirting back at him. It had always seemed to be a bit of a game, because I had grown up with it."

Anna glanced over at her mother who was serving cake at the end of the table and watched her almost flinch as if she had been hit, each time her husband touched another woman. "Suddenly I had some insight in what it was doing to her, watching her husband playing so visibly with other women like that. I became incredibly angry with him for treating her like that. Couldn't he see how miserable it made her?"

The crunch came when Anna's father started an affair with the divorced mother of one of the girls in her class. "My mother never said a word, just packed up our belongings the next day and we moved back to live with my grandparents. School was awful from that moment on – everyone knew about the affair, and compared my mom, who was dowdy and a little overweight, (and I now know, in a deep state of depression) with the new woman my dad had been playing with, who was a tall, dark beauty and great fun to be with."

Anna spent her teen years being angry with her mother for her resignation and giving up without even a fight, and absolutely livid with her dad for being so childish and self-gratifying, but never thought that it would affect her until she started dating.

"I would fly off the handle if my boyfriend so much as looked at another woman when he was with me, and if he spoke to someone that I hadn't met I would give him the third degree of 'who is she, where did you meet, how do you know her, do you think she's pretty, is she prettier than me…?' The litany was endless, but I couldn't stop it. I would try to control him and his activities, constantly checking up on him, and would never believe anything he said; I was suspicious and paranoid and manipulative."

For Stefan, who dated Anna, he couldn't believe how much she could change. "From being a vivacious, funny and vibrant being when we were alone together, she would morph in front of me into a spitting, controlling, paranoid bitch. I used to be terrified of bumping into a girl from the office while I was with her, or would cringe if the waitress who served us was young and pretty, knowing that was trigger enough to unleash her vicious spiteful tongue."

Programmed behaviour

For the most part, we don't connect our previous experiences and programming with our current behaviour. What on earth does the fact that I am jealous of my boyfriend's work colleagues, or insecure about the pretty young waitress serving us at lunch have to do with what happened on the playground, or arguments I witnessed in the home?

Surely the root of this problem is this event that I am dealing with right now, not what happened twenty, thirty, forty years ago? Surely what happened years before is not even relevant to this relationship I am in right now, but was an entirely different set of circumstances altogether.

The answer lies not in the current situation that is playing out right now, but in the emotion and mental thought process previous situations have created, and the response and belief that gets anchored, either through just one major experience, (or one that seemed major to the person at the time), or through repeated stressful exposures over a period of time.

The power of these beliefs is not just an engrained psychological programme however. It goes deeper, far deeper, until it becomes part of our cellular memory, part of our energy system, that until challenged *and healed*, becomes an integral part of our being.

The little girl who was very aware that her eyes were squint, and who was called four eyes and bug eyes, grew up not looking at anyone full in the face, so that they couldn't see just how ugly she really was. When other girls were experimenting with make-up and clothing, she stuck in the shadows, not calling attention to herself, because she had learnt and internalised at a very deep level that any attention was generally followed by teasing and humiliation. She felt desperately insecure and judged her looks to be inferior.

When she is now confronted with a glorious specimen of the female form as her husband's ex flame, with whom she feels she has to compete with for her partner's attention, she reverts back to that little nine year girl, with a patch on her eye, feeling inferior and insecure, and judging herself lacking. And the nine year pulls on her sense of self-worth that should have been instilled in infancy. But if that is also lacking, how does she respond?

Two completely different incidences, triggering exactly the same response. 'I am not good enough, I am inferior,' she says, and she withdraws again, back to the shadows where she cringes, waiting for the verbal attack of her physical body, for the teasing and humiliation.

Hopefully this time it doesn't come, yet the adrenalin is *already* surging through her body as her psyche remembers the onslaught she endured as a child, and unless she is critically aware of that inner turmoil as its happening, she will respond according to her programme.

Figure 6: Subconscious and programmed response to current episode

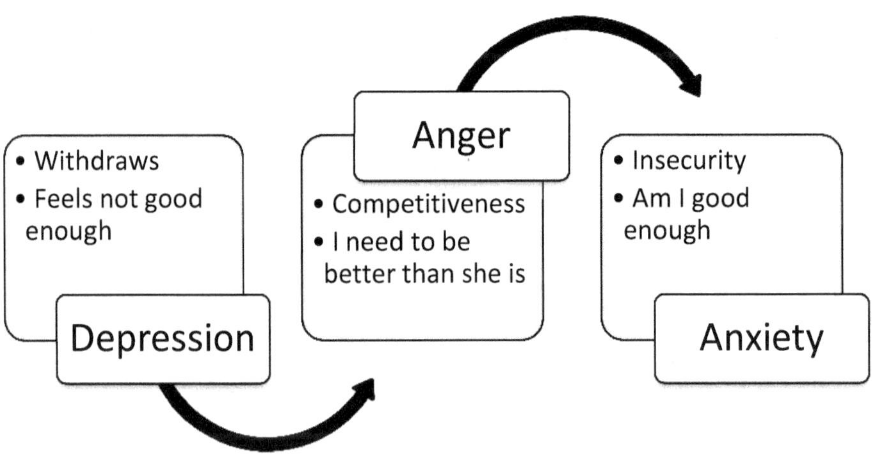

And this is just the tip of the ice berg!

When a current event or stressful situation happens now - like meeting up with a pretty girl from his office, or being served by a young sexy waitress (as in Anna's case), or listening to stories about how great his time in America was (as in mine), it is so easy to ride the wave of the emotions that are surging through you *at that moment*, instead of pausing and stopping to consider if their roots are really somewhere else entirely. Could they have been formed in our childhood, our woundings, our expectations of how relationships really work based on what we have lived through and witnessed in our formative years?

(Figure 7: Our conscious response to what is happening versus the hidden, unconscious motivations of our behaviour)

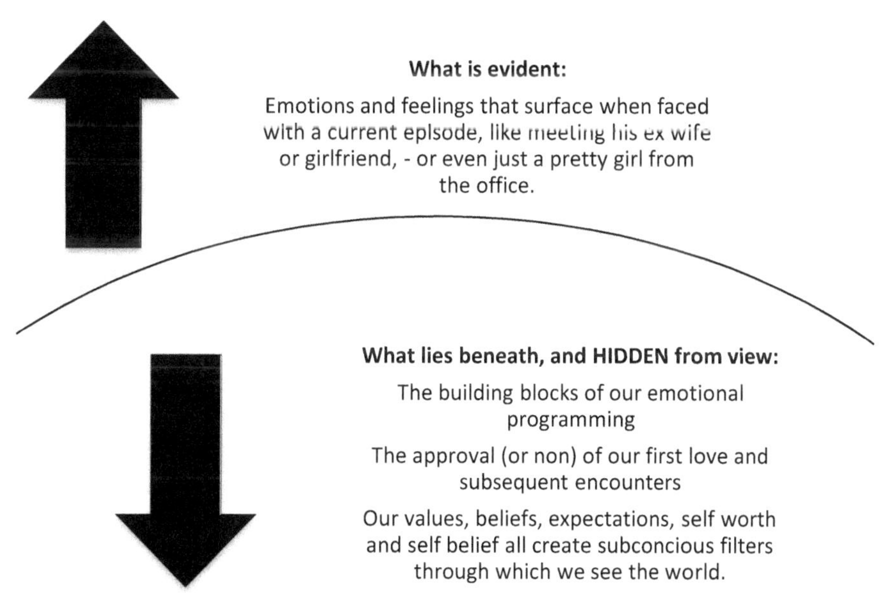

The Power of our Filters

I remember the first time I saw filters being used in photography. I was a young marketing assistant working for a large German automotive firm, and I had organised a photographic shoot of some of our newly imported product range. It was a very grey day, full of cloud cover and heavy skies, and I was worried that the trucks and tyres we were photographing would be dull and lifeless. I watched in amazement as the photographer fitted a series of different colour filters in front of the lens, and proceeded to take the most breath-taking photos. (Well perhaps breath-taking doesn't quite apply to trucks on a skid pan, but you know what I mean!)

He had managed to change the entire look and feel of the image, the perspective, the depth of the picture, simply by adding a filter.

How often do we do exactly the same, without really being aware of it at all?

Based on our life's experiences and understandings we have made certain decisions about our coping or survival strategy. We have reached our own inner conclusions about how 'life, love and everything else' is meant to work.

These perceptions *or filters* get locked not just into our emotional psyche, but also into our emotional and mental energy field by the sheer force of emotional intensity that accompanied the experience. These filters are so strong, so powerful, that an entire coping strategy and the subsequent belief system that becomes entrenched

Our emotional energy field literally begins to throb with this intensity, pulsating our message and belief system out into the world around us.

Thus that belief formed in high school "…men only want one thing, and there isn't a faithful man on the planet…" gets programmed into our energy field, which in turns throbs and broadcasts this message to the universe.

As we know, like attracts like, until all the men who are jerks, who do only want one thing and who are chronically unfaithful, respond to the siren call of our so-often subconscious belief system, and appear in our space, wanting of course, only one thing.

When we realise that this is what they expect, it disillusions us still further, intensifying our belief, making it stronger than ever before, and in the process, magnifying the pulsing, throbbing allure of our belief system.

And because our filter, our core belief, is that all men are jerks who only want one thing, we are effectively programmed to only recognise the jerks, only see what we expect to see.

We may not even consciously be aware that 80 year old Mr Jones, who lives downstairs and who every day holds his wife's hand tightly as they walk slowly round the park together, is a MAN, or that the boss, who has been happily married for 20 years is a MAN, or even that a much loved and respected brother who also adores his wife and would never cheat on her, is a MAN.

Our filters block out everything that doesn't match what we expect to see, and in some cases, adjust the landscape artificially to fit our internal belief.

Our filters are why two people in a relationship can see the same experience from two such completely different perspectives. "When I hold my wife and make love to her and tell her that she is so beautiful to me, it's because that is how she is for me. She is beautiful because I love her, and we share a common life and dreams and hopes together," says Franz.

But for Sue, *it has never felt true*, not because his words are insincere - *But because her filters do not allow her to receive the incoming information and match it with the belief system she already has in place.* Sue's entrenched belief, programmed from a very early age, is that she is not attractive, not desirable, and looks very different to other women. She hears the words beautiful and sexy, and tries to make them fit with what she already has decided is true. When they simply cannot be made to fit, she rejects them as Franz just trying to pacify her or make her feel better.

The first steps of a new dance, a new relationship ritual starts to emerge, where he tells her she is beautiful, but her energy rejects it because it conflicts with the "truth" she has already decided upon. And because of the discrepancy between his words, and her feelings, there is a 'sincerity gap' which ironically makes her feel even more insecure.

There is a lie in the words, says Sue, *because I cannot feel them to be true.* They do not resonate anywhere within me. I hear them and hold them up against my inner mirror, and have to reject them as they do not fit my internal image of me. And because he says words that are so patently untrue, that are such obvious lies, I start to feel insecure about the truth of the other things that he tells me, such as he loves me, I am the one he wants to grow old with, I am the love of his life.

If he lies to me on something as important to me as that, how can I trust anything he says to be truthful?

The moment of real enlightenment in this instance however, is recognising *the power of the filter at work as the lie,* not Franz's statement of beauty, or Sue's inferior belief about the way she looks.

The filter creates a chasm, a gap, between what is real and true and honest, and what is perceived and believed and internalised. When we can start to recognise that as the truth, we can begin to challenge the internal image or belief system, instead of the relationship.

Seeds, Soil, Sustenance.

For any comment, or event or episode to have an effect and trigger a response, there have to be three factors.

- There have to be *seeds*: A comment, a feeling of insecurity, an action that seems incongruent with what we believe the correct behaviour to be. The seeds are the external trigger from our partner, or from a situation, which triggers a deeply programmed, and mostly subconscious response in us.

- There has to be *fertile soil*: For the seeds to take root and start growing, in the fertile soil created from our previous experiences. Our programmed beliefs form our filters, which form our perceptions, which simply reinforce and strengthen those core beliefs.

- There has to be *sustenance*: Negative self-talk, negative self-image, lack of worth and value, which feed the seeds, and allows the plant to grow and flourish.

The plant flourishes, the roots dig down and tap into our self-doubt and worthless experiences, anchoring it strongly and attaching to our existing hidden identity.

The plant grows like a creeper, shooting out tendrils and wrapping around any joyful, happy experience, choking out all happiness and squeezing the life out of it. Left unchecked, (and fed by enough negative self-talk) this plant grows ever larger, hooking into any pleasurable experience and space in our lives, blocking out the sun, leaving us isolated and alone in the darkness.

Key Points of this Chapter

- ❖ This current situation that is making me feel insecure and jealous is simply the tip of the iceberg.

❖ The root of this distress and emotional response lies deeper within my childhood, teen and early adult years.

❖ We are approved and validated at various stages of our childhood development. If this approval is positive and worthful, then I achieve a sense of SELF and inner security about my self-worth. If this is negative and full of lack, then I struggle to form a strong sense of self, and become mistrustful of myself, others around me and my experiences through life.

❖ Our experiences in life create filters through which we view events and relationships, blocking out whatever does not fit our internal image of what we expect a relationship to be. Our filters are by our conditioning.

❖ These filters explain why two people can see and hear the same things, but understand and feel such very different emotions from the same event.

❖ Any current event needs seeds, soil, and sustenance in order to take root and grow – either into a positive and powerful event, or a negative and destructive reinforcement of core beliefs.

Self Reflection

1. What are my own key beliefs that I formed while growing up, during the various developmental stages?

2. What was my mother and father's relationship like, if I look back through my childhood eyes?

3. What does my internal security scale look like? Do I respond positively or negatively, as a general rule? How does this differ when I am feeling jealous or insecure?

4. What core beliefs have I developed through my childhood experiences?

5. Do I have filters on about how relationships work? If so, what?

6. What is my internal dialogue like? Is it positive and self-affirming, is it realistic and cognisant, or is it destructive and belittling and deprecating?

Chapter Six:

Hear It Roar!

I knew a man, who lived in fear, it was huge,
It was angry, it was drawing near
Behind his house, a secret place,
Was the shadow of the demon he could never face

He built a wall, of steel and flame, and men with guns to keep it tame
And standing back, he made it plain,
That the nightmare would never ever rise again
But the fear and the fire and the guns remain

It doesn't matter now, it's over anyhow,
He tells the world that it's sleeping
But as the night came round, I heard it slowly sound
It wasn't roaring, it was weeping,
It wasn't roaring, it was weeping.

Dan Heyyman, Performed by Bright Blue

As we reflect on our experiences and core beliefs that have been formed through the years, we begin to recognise the coping decisions we have made. Maybe we even start to understand the reasons why we made them, and the various strategies for surviving and success we have put in place over the years.

The child who felt insecure and ignored and invisible forms a core belief that she is unworthy and that her needs don't really exist, or if they do, that they are not important at all. Her inner dialogue echoes the subconscious messages she received while she was growing up:

"You are not important, for heaven's sake just shut up and stop whining, nobody gives a damn what you want, so just shut up and get on with it, you don't deserve it anyway." .

Her coping decision is to ignore that inner part of her that begs, pleads and screams for attention. She grows into adulthood, suppressing those inner feelings, refusing to acknowledge them or even accept that they exist, pushing them deeper and deeper into the shadows, until she has forgotten that they were ever born at the same time as she was.

When they burst out of her, in a rabid froth of criticism, accusations and scathing assumptions, leaving a wake of destruction and chaos behind, she is left just as shocked and devastated as her partner. It's a part of her that she never knew existed, and she is left powerless and defeated, not knowing how to cope with this "new" part of her.

One Life, Many Roles

We live many roles simultaneously in our lives, and sometimes it's hard to know when one role stops and another one starts, they overlap so much. At any moment in time, we inhabit at least four or more roles, and each of these roles speaks with a different voice.

As I write this to you, I am a wife; a mother; a lover; a housewife; a therapist; a friend; a daughter; a sister; an author – and each of these roles exist comfortably within me, and in co-existence with each other, as I switch effortlessly between taking a call from my mother, kissing my husband hello as he walks through the door at the end of the day, telling the kids that they've had enough TV and it is time for homework, and unloading the dishwasher as I start preparing supper. The voice that I use as I switch between these roles differs subtlety from the others; for example, the voice I use to talk softly with my husband at the end of a long day is not the same voice that I use when I am asking my children if they have got all the information they need for a project presentation the next day, and it's certainly not the voice I use when my mother calls to ask me whether she can come and stay for the summer holidays.

We are comfortable with this concept of multi-tasking, and role playing, because it describes what we all know to be true. I have many functions, many skills, many talents that I call upon when I need them ... my talents as a lover are not appropriate when I am organising the school breakfast buffet, and vice versa. My talents as a counsellor and therapist are not appropriate when dealing with my bank manager, or driving on the Autobahn.

These roles that I play do not demand that I deny the existence of a more menial role. For instance, the housewife in me knows that her job would not be as easy without the willing participation of the part of me who cleans the toilets, (yuck) or does the ironing (double yuck) or shovels the never-ending snow off the side-walk in winter. (This last part is enough to make me run for the hills, but wow, do I respect that part of me that does it).

There are certainly times when I feel that one part of me has had way too much attention to the detriment of the rest of us, like when I am running a workshop or training course, part of me is required to stand and speak, captivate and perform for hours, sometimes days at a time. There are times when it seems that all I have done for days on end is clean the house and climb up mountains of ironing. At times like that, the other parts seem to get together and whisper suggestions that maybe it's time for another part of me to dominate for a while.

And I listen. To the part of me that says, take the afternoon off, go shopping, relax, I promise her that once we have passed this deadline, that's exactly what we'll do. The part of me that wants a clean home with ironed clothes in the closet, interacts and negotiates with the part of me that needs to finish just another chapter, making a deal that works for both parties.

Sometimes, it's chaos. But mostly, it's ordered, and we all know what we're supposed to be doing, how we are supposed to be behaving at any given moment in time.

It's the same with everyone. And we all accept it because it's a non-threatening fact of life.

One Life, Many Voices

It is the same with our voices too.

Inside of me is the voice of the part of me who is secure, comfortable, safe in her relationship. The voice of the 45 year old woman, who has seen beautiful things in her life. The voice of the poet, the mystic, the soul on a journey toward God, the voyager, the believer, all co-exist and talk to the voices of my futures hopes and dreams, as well as the voices of my past experiences. (these experiences have many voices, sometimes speaking as a collective, sometimes as the individual experiences themselves).

The voice of a little girl who was scared, alone and frightened lives there; the child who didn't understand what was happening when her brother died, and her mother sank into a deep depression lives there too. Somewhere inside of me is the little girl who watched her parent's marriage disintegrate, and watched her father disappear, never to see him again.

So too is the voice of the child who learnt to suppress her needs, as she had to take care of her mother and little brothers, the child who became a chronic people pleaser, who learnt to deflect attention onto others by always being the one to take charge and look after situations. That little girl with bottle top glasses, becoming aware that she was considered very strange looking compared with the other little girls on the playground, jostles for space along with the part of me who believed that unless she was good, very good, and unless she worked really hard at keeping everything together and in place, that she was unworthy of love and attention.

(No such thing as a free lunch, is one of the core beliefs that came out of suppressing that voice).

Somewhere inside of me is the voice of someone who is asking for reassurance that she is ok, and not finding an answer, pushes that voice away until it cannot be heard anymore, and who then believes that she is not lovable, not worthy of love.

Somewhere inside of me is a voice, crying, begging to be recognised and heard, because the very act of hearing of the voice would mean that I exist. It is drowned out by the voice that says 'shut up, you are too ugly, not worthy of being heard, so shut-up, shut up'.

Or worse: "You are ugly, you are a monster, you are despicable and huge and frightening, and you don't deserve to exist".

We build walls, and imprison those parts of us that have never been recognised, never been heard or validated, and like the world, we turn our heads away and refuse to listen to what it is they are saying, deep inside of us.

We police these hidden secret places within us so carefully, and so they can only ever come out when we let our guard down, when an event or episode is so overwhelming, so huge that it catapults back to the last time this voice tried to be heard.

Like the little girl standing on the playground asking why she never gets picked to play with the group, or the little boy asking to please be allowed to come inside the pub with his parents and have something to eat, while they are too busy drinking to remember their responsibilities, or the baby who lies crying pleading with her depressed mother to please love her and take care of her, our voices remain ignored, rejected, unheard yet again.

The SELF which was abandoned and rejected and ignored by those critical stages of our development gets the ultimate rejection as we ourselves abandon the very core of who we, again and again ... and again.

The Validity of the Voices

The first thing to realise here is that you are not going crazy when you admit that you have these voices clamouring to be heard inside of you.

Everyone has these voices inside of them; we all speak with different voices at different times, in the various situations we encounter during the day. Think for a moment of your daily routine.

You can have a massive argument with your partner before work, yet when you go into the sales presentation, you are speaking with the voice of a corporate professional. You can go to the school parents-teachers meeting, and have a meeting with the teachers and speak as a concerned and participatory parent, before driving home that evening. Walking into the kitchen, you pick up the argument where you left off when you bump into your partner coming home from work.

Everyone has voices, and explained in this way we can see how we move and interchange between each role, using a specific voice to negotiate and move through the various different situations we encounter during the day. It's easy to accept.

But somehow, saying that my emotions also have voices, my experiences also have voices, that the ignored and rejected parts of me have a voice just as much as the voice that deals with the boss, or with the school teachers, makes us feel a little unsettled. We don't want to explore that possibility because of the fear of, God forbid, finding out that we are a candidate for the funny farm, or that we should have had a starring role in the movie Sybil, or The Four Faces of Eve.

So let me hasten to reassure you, I am not talking about multiple personality disorder, or personality dissociative disorders; these voices are a normal, natural, and valid part of us, and clamour for recognition, for attention. They demand to be heard.

The problem, of course, is obvious. Our conditioning as we are growing up, through the primary and secondary encounters, teaches us and reinforces in us which voices are acceptable, desirable, worthy, and which are not. Society teaches us that we have to hide away any energy or action that is negative, destructive or ugly, and encourages us (and insists in many cases) that we do not show what society deems to be undesirable.

Stand up and talk about sex (and masturbation even) and you will have a willing audience. Talk about any deviant sex fetish you may need help recovering from and society refuses to listen. You can go on TV, or appear in a magazine, discussing your drug addiction, your obesity problem, your drunkenness – but don't show us what you look like when you are smoking your crack pipe, or gorging yourself on food, or throwing up in the gutter from consuming too much alcohol. We don't want to see that side of it, don't want to witness the power of destruction, because it is just too ugly to contemplate or consider, that faced with different choices or different experiences, that potential or possibility also exists within me.

It's the same with insecurity, and jealousy. We don't want to hear about it, don't want to hear your clinging, desperate, pleas for assurance, we don't want to watch your mouth curl when your hurl out vicious criticisms, or sarcastic accusations. We don't want to be witness to your insecurity.

It's undesirable. We want to hear the success stories of the person who has conquered their drug addiction, not the desperation and despair of the person who will do anything for another fix. We want to applaud the size 4 model who has beaten her bulimia, but not be forced to watch as she sticks her finger down her throat to vomit up her last gorging binge.

Having learnt our lessons really well of what is acceptable in polite society (and especially in a relationship), we do to ourselves what society does to us - we ignore the voice of our insecurity and jealousy, driving it underground, denying its existence completely.

Listening to the Voices

Until we allow all our voices to be heard, until we *listen, really listen* to what it is they are asking for, we will not heal. What the voice is asking for is validation that it exists, that it is worthwhile, that it is part of you.

It's frightening to allow ourselves to listen to the voice, and to allow ourselves to *hear, really hear* what it is trying to say to us, because we have witnessed it in all its self-destructive power. We have watched its manipulation and criticism, its depression and anger, its craving for reassurance. Surely if we listen to it, we will be raising all of those emotions up to the light, making them more present in our lives, not less?

But, in refusing to listen to them, we inflate them into something demonic, something powerfully destructive, something ugly, sinful and disgusting. It is only in listening to the voice that we can even begin to understand for the first time that it is not the 'me, now' that is damaged. It's that part of me, way back when, that was damaged, so that the 'me, now' in this time, cannot hear or respond to what is truly being said.

A coping decision was made way back then, and a strategy put into play; filters and core beliefs came into existence, all because of that part of me that was damaged as I was growing up. It hears only what it is capable of hearing, through the filters and core beliefs, not what is truly being said.

The trick, then, is to find out which part of you is damaged and hurt, and what it needs in order to heal. This means that you have to allow yourself to follow the emotion, to witness it.

When the world says: 'stop being jealous' we are always trying to swallow it all down, with an immense effort, feeling bloated and swollen with negative emotion.

But what would happen, if instead of stopping being jealous, as we are told to, we allowed the emotion to unfold so that we could witness it, instead of being trapped inside it? To watch it? To talk to it and ask it what it needs?

When we hear ourselves saying to our husband or wife, "But you don't love me enough," what part of you is really whispering to you *but you have never loved me enough?*

When we beg for our partner to see me, to validate me, to make me feel visible and noticeable, what part of us is really saying *but you have never noticed me, I have always been invisible?*

When we cry and plead and say please choose me, please don't leave me, please love me, which part of us is asking to be chosen, asking to be loved, asking not to get left behind and ignored?

The Eastern Mystics tell us; As within, so without. Our behaviours, beliefs and actions, even the words and the voices we use to others, are simply a mirror of what is happening inside.

Following the Voices

Therapists and relationship counsellors will tell you that you must have a constructive and open dialogue with your partner in order for your relationship to flourish. I agree that this is vitally important, but believe it is only the second rung on the ladder of a healthy relationship framework.

The primary step, the most important dialogue you will ever have, is with *yourself.* An honest, no holds barred discussion with these different voices inside of you, the good, the bad, the ugly and the destructive, to find out what they need, what they crave, what is required to heal them.

We have ignored them for such a long time, and STILL THEY FIND A WAY OF BEING HEARD!

We have pretended they don't exist, yet they STILL have the power to create enormous pain and conflict in our lives, and destroy our relationships.

Clearly, ignoring them and pretending they don't exist, DOESN'T WORK, and it is time to try an alternative recipe.

Remember Anna from Chapter 4? Her father had had an affair with the divorced mother of one of her class mates, an event that became humiliatingly public for her. Throughout her parents' marriage Anna could not remember her mother speaking about her husband's flirting or serial womanising. "Almost as though by ignoring it, she could pretend that it wasn't happening at all," reflects Anna, 20 years later.

Anna's relationships however, are now suffering. Consumed by suspicion whenever her boyfriend even speaks to another woman, Anna flies into a jealous rage at the drop of a hat.

When we stop to follow Anna's voices, it's interesting to see what emerges.

Anna when provoked or insecure, screams in a loud jealous voice at her boyfriend:

> *Who is she, how do you know her?*
> *Why are you talking to her?*

Focus on that feeling of jealousy, that voice of jealousy. Who is saying these things, and what are they feeling in that moment?

> *I AM ANGRY, SO VERY ANGRY*
>
> *I want to shout at him for looking at her, for noticing her, for being so nice to her*

If we tune into that feeling of anger, that voice of anger, ask the ANGER what it is feeling right now?

> *I AM FEELING SO INSECURE*
>
> *Because she is pretty, very pretty, and anyone could see that it is so. What if he looks at her and thinks that he would prefer to be with her because she is so pretty. What if he looks at me and thinks that I am not attractive enough? I want him to reassure me that he won't leave me for her.*

And if we follow that voice that needs reassurance, that wants him to say he finds you attractive enough to stay with you?

> *I FEEL BEWILDERED, CONFUSED*
>
> *I feel bewildered and confused that I feel compared to someone neither of us even knows, how crazy is that... we don't even know her, the most he could feel is a physical appreciation of her, which is normal isn't it?*

So, following that voice that feels compared, that part of you that feels if you were to be compared with her, that you would be found wanting?

> *I'M AFRAID, I HAVE FEAR*
>
> *I am afraid that if he compares us that he would choose someone else over me, that he wouldn't choose me.*

Have you ever felt that way before?

> *OH YES*
>
> *Laughing bitterly … This is the way it went with my last two relationships, it was what broke us up each time. I'm afraid that this relationship is going the same way and there is nothing I can do to stop it.*

Can you remember a time in your childhood or early teen life when you felt this way as well?

> *YES*
>
> *When I was 11 years old and my dad chose to move in with my classmate's mother. She used to come to school on a Monday and tell everyone all the great things that they had done that weekend, with my dad. He was my dad, and he chose to be with her.*

Was there ever a time before that?

> *YES*
>
> *Dad flirted all the time, with any woman who was around, and now that I think about it, he was always spoiling their daughters too, calling them 'his little princess' and playing with them. I think it was his strategy for impressing their moms, but I was supposed to be 'his little princess' and he would push me aside whenever a pretty mother with a daughter came by.*

How did that make you feel?

> *INVISIBLE, NOT THERE, NOT EXISTING*
>
> *He never came to see if we were ok, he never tried to sort things out with my mom, never acknowledged that we were his family.*
>
> *My class mate became 'his little princess' I suppose, and just stepped into my shoes. I was instantly forgettable, imminently replaceable.*

And that made you feel?

WORTHLESS, NOT WORTH FIGHTING FOR, NOT NEEDED

It hurt so much. He just left us all, just abandoned us all. Walked away without a backward glance. If I think about, I became suspicious of anything people said after that. If I couldn't even trust my dad to fight for me and want me, then who could I trust?

So when you have a jealous attack and get angry and vicious with your boyfriend for smiling at the pretty waitress, what is your jealous voice really saying to you?

IT'S SAYING THAT IT WILL PROTECT ME FROM BEING HURT AGAIN

It will protect me from feeling that hurt again, from feeling compared to someone else. It will try to protect me from feeling so insecure, frightened, invisible and worthless.

Is that a good thing or an ugly thing that this voice is trying to do?

IT'S A BEAUTIFUL THING

It's just trying to protect me and keep me safe

What is that jealous voice trying to say to your boyfriend when you have a jealous fit?

IT'S SAYING ...

Please don't hurt her, she's been hurt enough. She doesn't need to feel that way ever again.

It is only when we give ourselves permission to acknowledge that the voice is really there, and then to follow it and listen to what it is trying to say to us, and be patient enough to have a dialogue with it, that we can begin to find out where the true wounding lies. With Anna, the wounding is not with her 31 year old self, who reacts negatively to any woman her boyfriend speaks to. The wounding was in a little girl, in the primary phase of her conditioning, watching her father betray her and her mother again and again, up to the age of 11. The wounding was compounded by her secondary reinforcers, who then teased, mocked and humiliated her, judging her and her mother as lacking when compared with the dark haired beauty and her daughter that her father chose over them.

The coping decision made at that age was to become suspicious, with a core belief of ´I cannot trust anybody. Even my own father didn't want us and chose someone else´.

And the survival strategy that became cemented in place was to fly off the handle whenever a pretty woman entered the equation, in protection of a little girl who needed to be protected all those years ago, - and wasn't.

Plea for Acknowledgement

The voices that we use with our partners and spouses, of jealousy and insecurity, are masking feelings and emotions on the deepest level of invisibility, non-existence, non-worth. But these feelings are so silent, so hidden that they have no voice, and so use the voice of jealousy, anger, criticism, pain, insecurity to speak up for them.

It takes a brave soul to acknowledge that these feelings are there, that they do exist, hidden within the depths of non-self, non-worth, non-identity.

It requires courage to allow yourself to listen to what these voices are trying to say to you, with each jealous or insecure episode.

It is a vital step toward healing, and to validating those parts of you that have invisible for so long. By giving your innermost experiences a voice, we suddenly start to see that they were trying to protect us, not destroy us, all along.

Key Points of this chapter

- ❖ We play many roles simultaneously throughout our lives. I can consciously be a wife, mother, friend, daughter, therapist, effortlessly flowing from one role to another.

- ❖ I use different voices to communicate, depending on which role I inhabit at the time

- ❖ It is the same with my emotions and past experiences. They too, have voices, whether expressed or unexpressed, that live within me, and with enough of a trigger, they will manifest.

❖ These voices cry for acknowledgement, for recognition that they exist. To deny and ignore them can create destructive consequences that leave us bewildered and confused by our emotions and behaviours.

❖ Everyone has these voices; I am not going crazy when I acknowledge the voice of my insecurity and jealousy, nor giving in to it. I am empowering myself when I begin a dialogue with myself.

Self Reflection

1. What roles do I play right now in my life, and what voices accompany these roles?

2. What voices are there inside of me as a result of my childhood experiences and understandings?

3. When I have arguments with my partner as a result of my insecurity, or I withdraw into depression, what voice am I using then? Have I ever felt this way before?

4. What is this voice trying to say now? Am I willing to allow myself to listen to the voices deep inside of me?

Chapter Seven:

Feeding the Beast

We discover the most vital clue to healing our jealous and insecure nature is ironically not by doing what our conditioning tells us to. Healing lies in going against the grain, in swimming against the current, and listening to *what is*, instead of what we have been told *should be*.

We discover that our words of anger, anxiousness or depression that burst up and out of us, are just masking a deeper energy that has lain invisibly alone for too long. Simply by acknowledging that it exists, that it is a part of us, regardless of how it got there, we are allowing it to breathe a huge sigh of relief at last.

"I exist," it whispers. "Finally, I am visible."

Acknowledging its existence, however, is not enough.

Understanding why it came into being in the first place is not enough. It's a step in the right direction, but it is not enough to satisfy this part of you and the need for validation, comfort and healing.

Understanding why I behave this way, why I fly off the handle is not enough to stop it from happening again. It may explain my behaviour; it doesn't excuse it.

If we want to heal, truly heal, we need to walk forward into even more uncomfortable territory to claim our healing – and in so doing, finding the power of our inner self along the way.

Simply a coping mechanism

As we examine our coping mechanisms and strategies we have put in place with our new awareness, we start to see the holes and flaws in how they have failed us, and what they were trying to protect us from in the first place.

Figure 8: Coping Mechanisms

COPING MECHANISM	FLAW / PROTECTION
Withdraw, hide away, deny, ignore	Core Belief: I am unworthy, I deserve this pain. Protection: If I don't acknowledge it, it doesn't exist. My pain from previous experiences cannot hurt me any longer if I do not validate it. This pain cannot hurt me if I don't allow myself to see it. If I hide away and withdraw from the pain, it won't follow me. Flaw: As I withdraw away from the pain of previous experiences, and ignore and deny the pain that each flare up of jealousy causes, as I ignore the triggers in my current life that fuel my insecurity, I reinforce within me that I am not worthy. I deserve this on some level, otherwise it would not keep happening to me.
Walk away from the argument, or in extreme cases walk away from the relationship	Core belief: You are going to leave me anyway. Everybody always does, sooner or later. Protection: If I walk away from the argument I refuse to give any part of me a voice, and I can continue to deny the existence of anything other than what is apparent. You are going to leave me anyway – everybody always does, so I will leave you before you

	leave me.
	Flaw: As I walk away from the situation or my partner, I repeatedly walk away from that part of me that is begging for a committed action of staying. I effectively walk away from myself.
Intense questioning, needing to know every detail	Core Belief: If I know more, then everything will be ok. Protection: I have pain in my life because of lack of knowledge or lack of information, and I have had to make survival strategies based on this lack of information. If I can keep myself informed, I can protect myself, and not be caught unawares again. Knowledge is power. Flaw: As I keep questioning, I enter into a self-comparison and competitive phase where I take every answer and compare my own offering against it. If I feel superior, I become judgemental. If I feel inferior, I feel less than, a failure and not worthy.
Demanding resolution on my terms	Core Belief: I have to take charge of this situation to sort things out, I can't rely on anybody else to take care of me. Protection: I need to control the situation to know that I am safe in this space. I can only feel safe if I control all the moves. I have previously felt unsafe in my life because somebody else held all the power and I was manipulated to suit somebody else's needs. If I don't control the situation first, I will end up being controlled. Flaw: As I try to control every

	eventuality, I become manipulative and disregarding of other people's needs and feelings. I run the risk of doing exactly to others what has been done to me in the past.
Becoming weak, vulnerable, weepy, clinging, in need of protection and reassurance	Core Belief: I am nothing if you no longer see me. Protection: If you see how deeply this has affected me and hurt me, you will realise how important you are to me, and how much I love and need you. *(and / or)* I don't know what to do without you around, and I don't know that I will able to take care of myself. I am terrified at the thought of life without you and need to do anything to make you stay. Flaw: As I become more and more dependent on you, I push the notion of SELF further away until the core of who I am becomes practically unreachable and unrecognisable. *(and / or)* To keep you staying with me, I need to up the ante, and to escalate my need for you, until I enter the realm of emotional extremes or even emotional blackmail.
Becoming flirty, flighty, hyped up, manic good mood	Core Belief: I have to put a face on how I really feel, it is not safe to show my feelings. I am only desirable when I am behaving in a certain way. Protection: If you are having a great time with me you will stay with me. If I behave in a good mood all the time, becoming a little manic and overly

	demonstrative, you cannot see how this is affecting me.
	Flaw: As I become better at putting a 'face' on it all, I hide my emotions away from myself, and push them further underground.
Becoming critical, suspicious, vicious, sarcastic, word sword-play	Core Belief: I cannot trust anyone.
	Protection: By becoming verbally abusive of you and your activities, I am protecting that part of me that has felt powerless and unheard in my past. Nobody ever tells the truth, and so, I am suspicious enough of you to double check what you are doing and to follow you, I can always maintain the upper hand and retain the illusion of power.
	Flaw: Because my filters and ingrained belief is so strong that 'everybody lies, and no one is ever faithful', I cannot hear, see or even begin to recognise that it is MY filter that is in error, not my partner's actions. I seek to blame external factors to rationalise why I keep feeling so miserable.
Physical loss of control, e.g. ripping of the buttons off his shirts, driving his car into the pool, wrecking his house or office	Core Belief: I have to maintain a tight lid on my emotions and feelings all the time. I can only express the damaged and hurt parts of me when I lose control completely.
	Protection: I protect myself from the enormity of the truth by losing control of the moment and myself, so that I do not have to deal with it. By wreaking destruction in my environment I keep the attention on the here and now, and not on my past pain and insecurity. (plus, if I wreck your car, you cannot go and see her, as you have no car to

	drive there in).
	Flaw: My pain is so overwhelming, so huge that I keep pushing it away, and compounding it with very real acts of destruction. I am deflecting attention off myself which is just too painful to deal with, and onto you with acts of "Look what you made me do".
Reciprocating in kind If you can, so can I!	Core Belief: If you don't want me, then I need to find someone who will. I am invisible without someone to validate me.
	Protection: If I think that you are paying too much attention elsewhere, then I will show you that others find me attractive and desirable. If you are spending too much time outside the home, then I will too so you know what it feels like. Translation: If I can make you feel as jealous as I do, you will pay more attention to me.
	Flaw: By focussing my attention away from the relationship and the problem, I am compounding the issue and delaying resolution and healing. Too wrongs in this case, can never make it right.
Drugging, drinking or some other obsession, negative activity to drown out the voices or thoughts	Core Belief: I need to hide away from this.
	Protection: By filling my mind and energy with some other (obsessive) activity, I leave no space for thoughts of either the current event, or the memory of past experiences to penetrate. If they cannot penetrate, then they do not exist, at least for a time, and I can (sort of) function.
	Flaw: What I don't realise is that I am

	not functioning well at all. By drowning out / blotting out / forcing out the pain and insecurity, all I am doing is delaying the moment when I have to deal with it. I cannot live in this no-man land forever. *(and)* Alcohol and tranquilising drugs suppress the central nervous system, precipitating an even deeper depression and personal collapse.
Punish self, through self-denial, self-mutilation, self-loathing, self-sabotage	Core belief: I am bad. Protection: I am obviously bad, obviously all of this is my fault, and I need to be punished in some way. If I punish me before you get to me, it will be easier all round. I don't want your punishment, it will hurt me even more than I am already hurting, so let me do it to me myself. Flaw: By punishing the self that is crying out for love and validation, I am simply pushing it deeper underground, and forcing it even further into the shadows, until healing becomes an even harder, more self-torturous journey than it needs to be.

Merle is a large woman, full of life, gorgeously vivacious and abundant, with long flowing hair and an infectious laugh. She has battled throughout her life with her weight, and only when Brian entered her life did she seems to finally accept her size and embrace life fully. However, when he left after years of loving her and providing her with the energetic security she needed, her hold on self-acceptance vanished overnight. She obsessed endlessly about the younger woman he had taken up with, googling her, looking her up on Facebook and comparing herself endlessly. The new girlfriend was young, taut and toned, while Merle was very aware of her unconditioned body and cellulite. In a fit of self-loathing, she took a knife and cut her thighs, breasts, and arms again and again, scarring her body badly. "It didn't even hurt that much," she confesses. "It couldn't take away the pain that filled the place where my heart used to beat."

Merle's coping mechanism is *PUNISHMENT and SELF LOATHING.* She has been so used to looking at herself through other's eyes, that she lost all identity as a worthwhile beautiful creature when Brian left. Instead she could only see herself as ugly, reinforced by the fact that he had taken up with a beautiful young woman immediately after he had ended their relationship.

Michelle grew to despise and hate her husband during their divorce, as he repeatedly let her and her son down, telling lies about his finances to avoid paying maintenance for his child, and denying a long term love affair that everyone else seemed to know about. It seemed that there was no area of her marriage to him that had been true. Now in a new relationship with a photographer, she is increasingly suspicious of her new lover and his projects with beautiful models, demanding endless details about the photo shoots, going through his pockets and examining his shirt collars for tell-tale lipstick or make-up marks. *Her core belief is that I cannot trust anyone.*

Maria grew up watching her mother crucify her father again and again with accusations of infidelity and wrong-doing. "My father was such a gentle man, so full of respect and compassion, and these qualities characterised his dealings with everyone. It used to enrage my mother when my father was kind or respectful to another woman; she wanted my father to ignore every other female on the planet, and to only focus on her. She couldn't understand that it was just not in his nature to be rude to people, not even to please her."

Maria grew up hating the way her mother castrated her father's energy, and feeling sorry for this man who simply tried to keep the peace.

"She had on-going arguments and feuds with most of the women in the family as well. For years, we were never allowed to speak to my father's sisters and their daughters, for some small incident that got blown up out of all proportion. "

Since leaving home, she has bent over backwards to always be kind, gentle and respectful with her partner. "I never question, never ask, never demand any information or evidence, pushing away any twinge or suspicion that I feel, because I refuse to behave like my mother." Maria's coping mechanism is *DENIAL*.

Christina's mother became caught up in the Christian church while she was growing up, eventually studying theology and becoming a minister. The family moved towns often, as Christina's mother followed her 'calling'. Her mother remembers doing God's work, Christina on the other hand remembers her mother always been available for everyone else but not for her family. While she was at high school, her mother accepted a missionary post in a rural country, helping to set up churches, schools and infra-structure there. Without question it was not an environment for her family or children, and so it was decided that Christina, her brother and sister would stay with her dad, and continue attending school, while her mother went off to 'work for the Lord'.

The marriage survived this unorthodox arrangement, and the children seemed to grow up strong and happy. Christina, however has never had a long term relationship. Beautiful and vivacious, she has no trouble attracting men to her side. The minute a moment of discomfit or conflict arises into the relationship, she packs her bags and leaves, as she has done so many times before in her formative years, and also, as she has observed her mother doing time and again. Her coping mechanism is to *WALK AWAY*; her core belief is that you are going to leave me sooner or later, so I might as well get out of this relationship first. It hurts less to be the one who leaves rather than the one who is left behind.

So now what?

Understanding the core beliefs that I have built up and the ensuing coping mechanism I have put in place is all very well and fine, but what do I need with it now? I can understand that the voices and reaction I employ are there to help protect and guard me for further hurt. How do I heal the inner sense of self, so that I can put these terrible emotions of turmoil, lack and invisibility to bed once and for all?

Trying to resolve the issue of insecurity that flares up in a relationship is like trying to pacify a hungry baby with a dummy. The baby screams and cries, and stops crying when you put the dummy in his mouth, but after a few hungry sucks, starts to cry even louder when he realises that no sustenance is forthcoming. He is starving and will protest constantly, until he is fed. Only then can he relax and calm enough to quieten down and sleep.

The only way forward is to find out what the hungry voice deep inside of is starving for - and having found what it needs to feed on, we need to let it feed. Only then, will it relax enough to calm and find inner peace.

As we have already discovered, if we ignore it, it does the only thing it can. It feeds off us, cannibalising us slowly and surely from the inside, leeching all joy and happiness from our lives.

The Sum of our Parts

We can accept that we are the sum of all our parts. There are many roles that we play, at any one time, sometimes simultaneously, overlapping each other, sometimes consecutively, a constant dance of roles and capabilities and appropriate behaviour by the right part of us, at the right time.

Each role has a specific voice, as we move effortlessly, and without thought into each role, and we can accept this too.

What is also true is this: Inside of you co-existing sometimes visibly, sometimes ignored completely, are younger versions of you, together with the experiences you encountered and the belief systems and coping strategies that were formed at that time.

Inside of me right now is the bewildered little girl who struggled to come to terms with her parent's broken marriage; the sobbing child who watched her father drive away after her brother had died is still standing at the front door in confusion. She has a voice, as we have already discovered. The part of me who sat on the playground praying that the other kids would either let me play, or ignore me completely, still sits there trapped in a cringing plea. The capable girl who grew up too quickly and took charge of everything as her mother sank into a deep depression, who compulsively organised, tidied, cleaned and looked after is still there doing her job. In fact she has done her job so well, that she managed to get the rest of me to grow up safely by pleasing other people, constantly trying to organise life (mine and others) so that life would continue to be safe.

(I think she is the reason I became a nurse, the reason I studied psychology and healing, the reason I am a counsellor and healer).

Once more into the breech

This step is critical. We need to go back to where we left off with our internal dialogue with the voices, where we recognised finally what the voices were trying to say to us. With Anna, when we followed her accusatory, sarcastic voice, she realised that it was actually hiding voices of bewilderment, hurt, confusion, invisibility, worthlessness.

Now, we need to go back to that space, and discover WHO is saying them. They are not just disembodied voices shouting into the wind, they belong to a younger, more fragile, more vulnerable part of you.

Remember that Anna's current voice in a relationship is screaming, jealous, accusatory, sarcastic; we only have to scratch a little way beneath the surface, before we found that this voice was actually driven by the voice of anger, bewilderment and insecurity. (the core emotions of jealousy). When we followed those voices we came to the voice of fear.

Remember we asked whether she had ever felt that way before, and Anna replied: "When I was 11 years old and my dad chose to move in with my classmate's mother. She used to come to school on a Monday and tell everyone of the great things that they had done that weekend, with my dad. He was *my* dad, and he chose to be with her.

And

"Dad flirted all the time, with any woman who was around, and now that I think about it, he was always spoiling their daughters too, calling them 'his little princess' and playing with them. I think it was his strategy for impressing their moms, but I was supposed to be 'his little princess' and he would push me aside whenever a pretty mother with a daughter came by."

Underneath the voice of fear was a very real emotion of: *invisible, not there, not existing.* "I was instantly forgettable, imminently replaceable" has become one of Anna's core beliefs.

And so this is our starting point:

Anna, if your life story had to be made into a TV movie, and you had the chance to see this encounter played out in front of you on the screen, what would you be seeing, as you looked at that remembered scene? Who would be there?

> *DAD being childish and charming, no responsibility. MOM, standing in the background, just watching, not saying a word. My BROTHER, slamming out the door with his soccer kit, refusing to be part of it.*

Are you in the scene?

> *I am there as well.*

What is going on?

> *Dad is trying to make light of the situation, make it appear less serious and dramatic than it so obviously is. He's promising that we'll still see each other, still have fun, but we all know him so well, know that he means to do it, but he'll just never get round to it. He looks so young, such a little boy. They got married so young, my mother fell pregnant with my brother when she was only 16. He never had a chance to grow up before he was supposed to be responsible and a father. He really is a spoilt little boy who just never grew up.*
>
> *Mom is standing there, in the shadows, not saying a word. She looks so old compared to him, as if all the worries and the cares of the world are on her shoulders. She looks like she went straight from child-hood into middle age, which I suppose she did really. Oh wow, they really were two complete mismatched souls, forced together because of the pregnancy. They should never have got married at all.*

Where are you?

> *I am standing there, begging him not to go. I am crying and clinging and promising to do anything, but please don't leave us. I've just got out the bath, and my hair is wet, and I am in my pyjamas which are too small for me. The tears are running down my face and I am begging him, but he's just keeps on packing his clothes.*

And then what happens?

> *He looks at my mom with a funny, weird look on his face ... he doesn't know what to say to her, and then ruffles my damp hair making it knot.*

He bends down and gives me a quick squeeze, and tells me that I will always be his number one princess, and he walks out the door.

And then what happens?

I run to the door of the apartment and follow him down the stairs, crying, begging, him to stay, but he doesn't look back, doesn't say another word, doesn't acknowledge me in any way. It's as though I am not even there.

And so Anna, stop that TV movie from running – pause the scene on that younger you, standing on the stairs outside your home, and in your mind, and heart, ask that younger you to walk out of the TV, and to come and sit next to you on the couch.

You can see how distressed she, how badly she needs to be comforted, and you also know now with the wisdom of being an adult, and because of your other experiences in life, that nobody was capable of hearing her or responding to her, comforting her in that moment.

Dad was too young to know what to say. Mom was too worn out and broken by her failed marriage to be able to reach out to you. Your brother has slammed out of the door, and you were all alone.

Ask that younger you to come and sit next to you on the couch, and give her what she needs the most. She needs to be held, comforted, loved. Take her onto your lap, and hold her close, and tell her you know how frightened and alone she feels. Tell her how brave she was for trying to get her father to stay. Kiss her and hold her and let her know how proud you are of her, for speaking out, when her mother couldn't.

Wipe her tears for her, and tell her she is not invisible, she is not worthless, she does EXIST, and that YOU heard her pleas to stay, and that you promise not to ever leave her alone again.

Tell her that you are sorry that she had to deal with this on her own for such a long time, but now, let her know that you are here, now to stand by her side and help her through this. She is not alone any longer because you are with her, and together you can get through this.

This little 11 year old girl needs to know a few things before she can get better.

- She needs to know that she survived this. At 11, sobbing on the stairs, she doesn't know that she will survive this, it is too overwhelming, too painful. You need to reassure her that she survives, and that she grows up, and she becomes a beautiful, competent, caring adult.

- She needs to know that she will be acknowledged and cared for, with love and visibility. Reassure her that this is so, and that you will always acknowledge her

- She needs to know that she became so strong that she made coping decisions and strategies, developing a core belief about how relationships need to work in the future.

- Tell her that you now know that she was doing this is order to *protect* herself from experiencing that kind of pain ever again.

- Let her know gently however, that her coping strategy was just as ineffective as her crying and clinging on the stairs that night. Trying to protect you on her own is not working. But together, with the voices of your other experiences, you might find a winning strategy that allows her to be visible, loved and trusted in a relationship.

- Thank her for being such a persistent part of your life, such an insistent voice, for not just disappearing and staying silent and invisible.

This is not an indulgent temper tantrum of a bratty adult refusing to grow up, or looking for excuses to explain why she becomes accusatory and sarcastic whenever another woman walks into the room. This is an act of compassion, understanding and healing from the part of you that craves a different relationship reality right now in your love affairs, your marriage, to that younger you that unknowingly held so much of the power.

By working cognitively with that younger you, you allow that hidden, deeper part to realise that the core belief and subsequent coping mechanism that was formed is *not working,* and that it is actually achieving the very opposite of what it craves, which is a) a healthy, strong loving relationship, and b) recognition and visibility that the younger part of you actually *exists.*

By extending compassion and understanding to that younger you, by allowing her to become visible and noticed, you begin a journey of healing that allows you to move into a healthier, kinder, fulfilling love relationship in the here and now.

By reassuring the child inside of you that her needs and pain have now been witnessed and understood and accepted, and that she no longer has to stand alone and frightened in this space, we start to move gently toward a space where healing can begin to take place.

Key points from this chapter

- ❖ We are the sum of all our experiences, whether we validate and acknowledge them or not.

- ❖ Acknowledging the voice is vital, but it isn't enough; we need to listen, really listen to what the voice is trying to tell us

- ❖ We form core beliefs as a result of our experiences throughout our life, and develop coping mechanisms as a result. Some of these coping mechanisms have a positive effect, whilst others are negative with far reaching implications into other areas of our life.

- ❖ The issue of insecurity that flares up in a relationship is almost irrelevant: Trying to pacify the now issue does nothing to pacify the hungry voice inside of you. In order to resolve the issue, we need to be prepared to explore the voice's needs, and then to give it what it wants.

- ❖ By working cognitively with ourselves, we provide ourselves with the very real tools for healing and recovery.

Self Reflection

1. What are my core beliefs? Are they protecting me or damaging me and my relationship in the long term

2. What hungry voices are trying to be heard inside of me? When I allow myself to listen, really listen to them, what are they saying? What do they need from me, or from others?

Chapter Eight:

Forgiveness

Almost there.

The next part of this vital healing journey is to extend that same compassion, understanding and healing towards those who played an unwitting part in the initial hurt and pain.

I say unwitting, because I really do believe that most parents (99.9% of them) will go out of their way to do the very best they can for their child. It is after all, a basic evolutionary driver, a deeply programmed impulse that moves us to look after and care for our children. By looking after and protecting our children, we ensure the survival of the species. More importantly we ensure the survival of our genetic line.

The problem of course, as parents, they are only able to do their very best with the tools they have *at the time,* and with the knowledge, awareness and information they have, *at the time.*

If we carry unconscious wounding from our childhood, if our emotional blue-print is scarred and hurt, is it possible that our parents suffer from their own filters, their own limiting beliefs, their own programming?

The answer is: *Of Course!* How can it be otherwise?

This realisation is critical in being able to move beyond the hurt and the pain of our growing up experiences. To recognise that our parents are also held trapped, stagnant, disempowered by their journey, just as much as we are by ours.

We go back to Anna, with that awful scene on the TV, from the last chapter.

When Anna suddenly realised that her parents were mismatched, that they had been forced into a marriage at the impossible age of 16, she understood far more that the pain she had suffered was an unintended side effect of a much bigger dynamic.

"I suddenly saw my father as he was; a father at 16, married to his first girl-friend. A kid who had never had a chance to go to parties, have fun with the boys and just grow up normally. While his old school mates were planning their prom night, or going out for a darts game, he was learning how to soothe a colicky baby. He never had a chance to flirt, or dance or have any of the normal teenage rites of passage," she said.

When she looked deeper, she realised that he came from a home life where there were no boundaries or parameters. His father had made his living driving trucks cross country, and so was always leaving his family behind for days at a time, whenever he went to work. This realisation hit Anna hard. "It's almost as if he was programmed from a toddler to leave, because he watched his father packing up and leaving for long periods of time. For a young child, it must have felt that dad simply disappeared."

As she looked deeper into her mother's journey, she consciously realised the impact of her mother's upbringing. "My mother had been brought up in an incredibly strict home, where her father dominated. He was actually the one who insisted that they get married when she discovered that she was pregnant. She had no idea how to challenge her new husband, and reverted to her childhood pattern, where the man did what he wanted and she had no say.

"At 26, where other people their age were just finishing university and settling down into marriage, these two people had been parents and working people for 10 years. I cannot begin to imagine how stifled they both must have felt.

With this understanding and awareness, Anna was able to feel a deep compassion unfolding within her for the way her mother had just stood there, not saying a word, whenever her husband flirted with other women. "Instead of the overwhelming anger I had always held towards her, I begin to feel compassion and empathy for her. The disdain and resentment I had built up between us began to melt as I realised that she behaved in the only way she knew how, and that she deserved my compassion and understanding, not my rage. She was disempowered and voiceless, but had always been so since her childhood. That was her emotional blueprint, and she was expressing herself the way she had been trained to do, all her life."

Likewise when she encountered her father again, as he ruffled her hair and promised that she would also be his number one princess, she felt overwhelming pity for the man who had never had an opportunity to make his own life choices, but was forced instead in marriage and a blue collar job.

"I realised in a blinding flash of clarity that as he walked down the stairs and out of my life, that he was not ignoring me, he was not discarding me. For the first time in the past 11 years, he was trying desperately to reclaim himself. He was crying his eyes out, but he had no idea of how else to let himself exist, unless he walked away."

And how could that be otherwise? He had watched his father walk away from his family, from him, all his life. The emotional understanding of why his father left the family all the time is not present in a two or three year old ... and by the time the child is old enough to understand the reason why dad goes away each time, it's too late. The emotional body has been charged, the pattern has been established, a belief system firmly in place: "Dad's leave".

And so Anna, can you, in the here and now:

- Go toward the man that your father was in that TV scene, and hold him, and extend him this compassion?

- Tell him that you understand what he is doing and why.

- Let him know that you see his need to reclaim his life, and you will honour that need. The way he did it may have been destructive or counterproductive, but can you honour the need that was the impetus for his desperate action?

- Forgive him for behaving in the way he did, knowing and understanding now that all he was doing was dancing his pre-programmed steps of his own private dance?

Can you also:

- Go and take your mother's hand where she stands in the shadows, and tell her that you understand why she remained so silent, why she was unable to find any words to say?

- Empathise with her lack of action, with her reticence to say anything, with her just standing and watching her husband leave, realising that she wasn't simply allowing him to go, she just didn't know that she was able to ask him to stay.

- Tell her that you are sorry that you became so angry with her coping mechanism, of denial and withdrawing away, and that the anger and resentment you felt was based on what you thought was going on, not on the reality of what really truly the case?

- Honour the person that she was, and feel compassion for the young woman who had never been allowed to see that she had any other choices in life?

- Honour that she coped with the entire situation – his flirting, his leaving, his affair – the only way she truly knew how?

- Forgive her?

True forgiveness of others demands that we start to see things (or at least be willing to try to see things) from their perspective, through their eyes – otherwise, all we are doing is making a judgement about their behaviour, instead of understanding the reasons why they behaved in that manner.

This is not about sympathy. It is about true empathy, putting yourself in their shoes, looking at their life experiences and understanding that the way they behaved, the coping mechanisms they put in place, their actions for good or for bad, is all an expression of their emotional programming.

As we do this, the filters that we have unknowingly put in place about our relationship with our parents, start to crumble, and we start to see them for who they are - and the reasons they took the decisions they did that in turn scarred us and set our patterns in place, so effectively.

But it goes deeper than that. From this new-found awareness that we are not the only ones who operate from a space of sub-conscious emotional programming, we stop seeing ourselves as victims or disempowered, but suddenly are able to see the filters and belief systems we have erected - and from this perspective, examine whether they still hold true.

Changing our Behaviour

As this new perspective starts to resonate within us, and we perceive that there are deeper levels of truth within the truth that we have always accepted without question, we experience a freedom within us.

We begin to move toward a place where we start to see the emotional programme for what it is - A PROGRAMME - and nothing more. As we challenge each level of the programme, with its beliefs systems, coping mechanisms and our subsequent behaviour we watch as it finally begins to crumble, shattering its hold on us, and liberating us to a space where we are consciously able, for the first time in our lives, to question whether it is a belief system that still holds true for us.

If the belief is still true, we are able to look at the way behave because of what we believe to be true, as in:

Anna had treated her mother with disdain and resentment throughout her life from that point on, because she believed that her mother had not even tried to keep her husband from playing around with other women.

Her new truth emerged as:

> *"My mother was incapable of fighting for her man and speaking out and saying what hurt her, or even what she wanted. Her voice had been silenced by her father years before, and the new truth that emerged was that she simply did not know how to. She didn't even know that she was allowed to fight for her husband."*

It changed the way she behaved with her mother from that point on. Whereas previously she would become exasperated and irritated by her mother's acquiescence and passivity, she now stopped trying to force her mother to say what she wanted, to make choices, to speak out, instead being far more aware of her mother's unspoken needs and compassionate when she dithered over the smallest decision. (Even choosing between having a toasted cheese sandwich or apple pie in a restaurant could take forever, a fact that before had irritated Anna to the point where she had refused to go out with her mom).

Her relationship with her father, which had deteriorated badly, is on the mend. "I no longer blame him for walking away, I no longer see him as a shallow jerk. I see him as unconsciously dancing his dance."

Forgiving yourself

Of course, part of the forgiveness process is that we extend that same level of compassion, understanding and forgiveness towards ourselves. It sounds so easy, but of course it is far easier to try to understand and forgive others, than it is to forgive ourselves.

We are hard on ourselves, sometimes brutally harshly intolerant and downright cruel to ourselves in a way we would never be to another person.

On a recent workshop I was running about Emotional Blueprints, a woman sat holding back the tears as she told us about her impending divorce. She was in deep distress, and at the prompting of one of the other participants, she haltingly began to tell her story, all the while apologising to the group for taking up so much energy, so much time, when we were all there for far more important things than hearing about her silly story. When the tears finally fell, she sat there, telling herself to "shut up, shut up, you stupid, pathetic woman".

I asked her gently if that was me crying whether she would tell me to shut up, that I was stupid and pathetic. Shocked she said, "No, of course not!"

What would you do, I urged? "I would hold you and try to help you, if I could see you were in pain," she said.

"Would you hold me and let me cry?" I asked her gently. "Of course I would," she said.

"So why can you not allow us to do that to you,?" I asked her. And when she couldn't reply, I asked her again softly, "Why can you not allow yourself to do that to you?"

She has two coping mechanisms in place: to deny, withdraw, ignore, hide-away from the pain, and then to punish herself with her negative self-talk.

Does she have a right to be upset and tearful? Of course she does, a divorce is a frightening, ground shaking event, and for her it is currently a very cruel reality in her life.

As she repeatedly tells herself how stupid she is, how pathetic and weak she is, she reinforces again and again how unworthy she is, how she deserves to be punished for even expressing her feelings; how truly unforgivable and unlovable she is.

And yet, it is the crux of the healing journey. To be able to look at others behaviour and forgive them is one thing. To be able to look at our life, to be objective and realistic about our life, to see each event, each experience as a building block of our Emotional Blueprint, is not easy to do.

It can be really hard to look at the journey our life has taken; but it is impossible to respect and honour each part of that journey, if there is no element of compassion, understanding and deep forgiveness toward ourselves.

But, bottom line, the bare cold truth of it is that unless you can move towards a place where you can:

- Enter into a dialogue with your inner voices and validate their existence inside of you, and listen to what they are trying to say.

- Accept the role that the different parts of you play, and that at times they act and behave in the only way they know how.

- Extend compassion and self-love to those sad, tragic or unresolved episodes of your life.

- Forgive yourself, for forming an entire coping mechanism and belief system.

- Forgive yourself for the years of (in an ironic, unconscious parody of your parent's life) denying vital parts of yourself.

- Understand why you were so suspicious and confrontational in your intimate relationships and forgive yourself for this current behaviour as well.

- And then forgive that younger part of you who acted so destructively, because you now understand that the intention was really positive.

Anna suddenly realised that the way she was behaving with her intimate relationships was because of her conditioning in her early childhood. "Because neither of my parents had been sarcastic or vicious with words, I just couldn't relate my behaviour with what I had learnt or observed from them. But this process made me realise that I was so deeply angry with my mother for not speaking up, and stopping my dad from playing around, and so, when it was my turn to have a relationship, I subconsciously behaved the way I thought she should have done. In the end it was just as destructive; I ruined every relationship with my constant paranoia."

This really is the crux of the healing journey:

Acknowledging what is

Allowing yourself to encounter those voices, those deep inner parts of you that have lain hidden and invisible for so long

Developing a dialogue

Gaining understanding, compassion and empathy For ALL Concerned

Forgiveness

And it is only once we have reached this stage of forgiveness, that we can begin to understand that there are alternative coping strategies, far more effective ones that will give us what we desire most of all: Love, attention, visibility and security.

Key points from this chapter

- ❖ It is a vital part of the healing journey to extend compassion, awareness and understanding to those who have played such a critical role in the formation of our emotional blueprint.

- ❖ 99% of parents do the very best they can for their children according to their own Emotional Programming; after all, we are genetically programmed as a species to ensure the survival of our young.

- ❖ Everyone does the very best they can with the tools and the awareness they have at the time

- ❖ Forgiveness is crucial, of the role that others have played in our past, but also forgiveness of the choices and beliefs we have made as a result.

❖ True forgiveness of others means being able to look at someone else's circumstances, and recognise their filters, their programming, their life experiences, with compassion. Once we are able to understand our past in the *here and now*, we are able to change our behaviour.

❖ We are far harder and more intolerant on ourselves than with others on our life journey. It is critical that we are able to sit in dialogue with those inner parts of us, and hear those inner voices, in order to find resolution and healing of the self.

Self Reflection

1. What are the life experiences of those who played the primary roles in the formation of my Emotional Blue-prints.

2. Can I see and understand the reasons for their behaviour toward me?

3. Does understanding of another's journey create compassion, awareness, recognition, empathy toward them?

4. Can I recognise and understand the choices and impetus for my behaviours? Am I able to extend compassion towards ME for my life decisions and behaviours, for my filters and coping strategies?

Chapter Nine:

The Lamb in Wolf's Clothing

Behind every behaviour is a positive intention

An important factor to realise is that behind every behaviour, every action, is generally (99.9% of the time) a positive intention.

We don't starve ourselves on a diet because we relish the feeling of being hungry; we do it because the very real reward at the end of it is being a dress size smaller for summer.

Following a gruelling study schedule for months before finals is hardly anybody's idea of fun, but we do it because the potential reward of a first class pass and career opportunities become a possibility with the hard work that we put it in now.

It is exactly the same with emotions and behaviour.

When we find behave in a certain way, it is because we are working from a deeper level of need that somehow gets met by that behaviour.

For instance, if I get up every morning and head off to gym, it's not because I am a gym junkie who thrives on adrenalin and pumping iron. It's because I have recognised that the behaviour (going to gym) meets a certain need (feeling emotionally strong and capable for the day).

Or if I force myself to speak to somebody every day in my excruciating German, (after a few years of planning and preparation, we finally made the move here two years ago. I am getting to grips with learning a new language, but it's hard going!), it is certainly not because I enjoy the looks of bewilderment and confusion my baby German inevitably invokes. Far from it. It is something that fills me with dread, and I can feel my heart begin to pound each time I have to speak to someone – yet I continue to do, simply because if I keep at it, and keep practicing every day, I know that I will eventually get my tongue around the sounds, and be able to communicate far easier. (Speaking German is a good skill to have when living in Munich, as you can appreciate!!).

We met Sandra briefly in Chapter 5. She found this process incredibly difficult. "How can I possibly forgive myself for wrecking homes by having affairs with married men, or for being so willing to let boys use me for sex during high school?" she fumed. "There can be no positive intention there, what I do is so awful."

(Can you see her coping mechanism at work? *I am bad; I deserve this at some level.*)

Sandra grew up in a house full of smart, intelligent women. Her mother was a career woman, highly successful in her profession as a finance broker; her grandmother had started a washing service, when her husband had been killed in the Second World War, which had rapidly grown into a chain of Laundromats across the country. She sold her empire for a handsome profit in her late 70's, and even now actively manages her financial portfolio on the stock exchange.

"There was no space for men in our home; mom and gran were always off working, and I would often come home to an empty house, 7 days a week," recalls Sandra. Naturally intelligent, with effortless good grades, she was however, immensely lonely, and comfort eating soon led to excess weight.

Thinking of her childhood doesn't bring back happy cheerful family memories. Instead she recalls the bleak, lonely times spent on her own waiting for her mother and grandmother to come home from work."

"I carried a lot of weight in high school, which I have since lost," she remembers. "I was not the kind of girl that boys would look at twice in those days. I didn't have many girlfriends either. School seemed to be divided into two types of girls – the pretty, popular girls who all the guys chased after, and girls like me, who stood on the fringe. I remember hating the pretty girls, all the while wishing I could be like them.

Talking it out

And so, Sandra what did you do to make friends and get out of the house?

> *I TRIED TO MAKE MYSELF ATTRACTIVE*
>
> *I hoped the boys would also ask me out, or the girls would want to be friends with me.*

And did they ask you out?

> *NO*
>
> *They didn't even notice if I lost weight or did my hair differently.*

How did that make you feel?

> *AS ALWAYS; NOT THERE, INVISIBLE*
>
> *It was ironic that someone as big and fat as I used to be could be as unseen, as invisible as I was. I remember walking into the room, and conversation would just continue, no-one would even notice that I had joined the group.*

And how did that make you feel?

> *WORTHLESS, LIKE I HAD NOTHING TO CONTRIBUTE*
>
> *I might have just as well been at home, staring at the same four walls and speaking to myself. I was so lonely most of the time.*

So what decisions do you make at that time?

> *TO MAKE MYSELF MORE VISIBLE*
>
> *It was around that time that the guys at school were all looking at the pretty skinny girls and talking about sex all the time, and of course, those girls had so many admirers, they could afford to play hard to get. I used to watch them playing their game of "look but don't touch, you can spend time with me but you can't have me" and be both irritated that they could get away with it, and envious that it seemed to just inflame the guys more.*
>
> *They got all the invites to the parties, and I never did. I remember feeling so jealous of them at the time.*

So how did you make yourself more visible?

> *I GAVE THE GUYS SEX, WHENEVER THEY WANTED*

I was with a group of guys and girls who were talking about Oral Sex, and how they would love to try it, when I heard myself say to one of the guys that I would do it to him if he wanted. Suddenly, all the boys in the group focussed on me, as if they were noticing me for the first time.

He took me into the boy's toilets, and I did a blow job on him there and then, even though I had never done that before. From that day on, all the boys suddenly knew my name, and I started getting invited to parties, and guys would come round and visit me. It always, always ended up in sex, I knew that if I ever said no that I would lose their interest in an instant.

How did the girls react?

LIKE I WAS DIRTY

Suddenly though I was the one who held the power. The guys would look at them, sure. But they would sit next to me, talk to me. It felt good to have their attention, and I felt like I was important, just as good as the skinniest, most popular girl. Better in some ways, because the guys couldn't get enough of me.

And how did that make you feel?

POWERFUL, VISIBLE

This was the price I had to pay for being noticed, I guess.

And did it sort out those feelings of loneliness?

YES. NO.

I guess the answer is yes and no. Yes, because now people knew who I was and knew my name, and I suddenly got invited to all the places. The girls hated me, but that didn't matter, I hadn't had girlfriends before anyway. The boys made sure that I sat with them, because they always knew I was game. It was heady stuff.

And no?

Because it always ended, and they would carry on with their lives and I would end up alone in that great big empty house again, with no-one to talk to. I got invited to all the parties, that was true. But the pretty girls got invited to meet the parents, or away for the weekend, or to the school dance, I didn't.

It's exactly the same now. I give the guys sex, and they go back to their lives, with their pretty wives and children, and I rattle around in this big empty apartment – and I am still on my own.

How do you react now?

I HATE THE WIFE AND KIDS

Without ever having met them, I hate them. I become scathing and sarcastic whenever he mentions his wife or family; here I am giving him what he wants ... sex on demand ... and the pretty girls still win. I still feel compared to someone else, and that they hold more power than me ... I might get to be powerful for a little while, but ultimately they hold the real power.

And how does that make you feel?

INSECURE

And jealous of everything they have and stand for.

Sandra, what is different about you at school and you now?

I HAVE CHANGED A LOT

I lost nearly 30 kg's after finishing school. I went to University, studied finance, and became a workaholic very much like my mother. I love what I do, and enjoy the thrill of international finance. I know that I am well respected, and considered to be one of the best in my field.

So do you still need the same strategy to attract guys into your life?

I HAVE NEVER THOUGHT OF IT LIKE THAT

Wow, that's interesting. In high school I was podgy and uninteresting, and had nothing to offer. Guys just were not interested in a fat girl with brains. Girls didn't like me, and I wasn't welcome into the girl cliques.

Now of course, it is very different. The fat girl with brains has slimmed down, and got a really good job that takes her all over the world.

I can look at myself objectively in the mirror and recognise that I am attractive.

The problem of course, is that because I have such a busy job, I don't have the time to spend in one place to cultivate a long term relationship, either with a lover or with a girlfriend, so I am still on the outside of the girl cliques, still on the outside with relationships.

I become really scathing and sarcastic when I hear of women in the office going on girl's nights, or out for lunches with their girlfriends. I have never had that, ever in my life.

In fact, I have prided myself on being a tough boss to work for, demanding and intolerant with my secretaries and assistants. When my last secretary told me she was pregnant, I viciously told her that women like her should never even try to have a career, as they obviously have no ambition and desire in life other than being a mother. I had her in tears, and she resigned later that week. At the time I felt justified, but what I have never admitted to anyone is that I would love to be in her shoes, with a loving husband and a much wanted baby on the way.

I guess I am still really lonely, only this time far better looking and accomplished.

Sandra's realised that she had put a behaviour strategy into place to deal with a very deep seated loneliness. Her 'bad behaviour' of trading sex for company – then and now - had not been because she was a marriage wrecker, or a slutty teenager. Giving sex increased her visibility, which meant that she was invited to participate in parties and school events. Increased visibility meant that she didn't spend as much time alone, which in turn meant that *she was not as lonely all the time* – just some of the time.

In the end, it became a vicious circle – she gave sex to feel less lonely. The next time she felt lonely, she gave sex, so that for a time she would feel less lonely. "I understand that it doesn't sort out the problem, but it makes me feel part of something for a short period of time, which is so much better than nothing," she says.

Her jealousy for the other girls at school, and now other women she encounters at work and in her adult life created two coping mechanisms

1. **Competitive:** I am always in a competition with someone else (in Sandra's case, the other women at the office, and the wife of her lover), and I have to prove that I am better in every possible way. The core belief of this mechanism is *that I have to be better in order to survive.*

2. **Demanding control:** I maintain the power through sarcasm, verbal conflicts, competitive energy, where I stay in control through vicious, scathing word fights. The core belief of this mechanism is *that I cannot trust anyone, and so cannot let my guard down for even a moment.*

Figure 9: Then and Now

THEN (as a podgy teenager)

Her behaviour:	Giving sex on demand.
The visible payoff:	To relieve the crippling loneliness of her empty life.
Her deeper need:	Inclusion to all the parties and events.
The invisible payoff:	Having somebody notice me, and talk to me, and spend time with me, so that I won't be as lonely.

NOW (as a sexy adult woman)

Her behaviour:	Giving sex on demand, scathing jealousy and vicious attacks on any woman in her space.
Her deeper need:	To relieve the crippling loneliness of her full, busy life.
The visible payoff:	Having someone to spend time with when I am not working.
The invisible payoff:	Having someone notice me and talk to me and spend time with me so that I am not as alone.

The process enfolds from this point, with awareness. When faced with the realisation that her behaviour was simply a sub-conscious strategy to try to solve that deeper need of loneliness and emptiness, Sandra was more able to extend compassion to that younger version of herself who had made the decision to give sex because she simply didn't want to be alone any longer.

"At that age, she had no idea of what else to do, and having tried it once, found that as strategies go, it was quite effective. It helped for a while," she said.

On the issue of her growing jealousy of other women:

> *"That younger me was lonely, and had no idea that what she really needed was friends, not sex. Up until that point where I starting giving sex to make friends, the other girls had not ignored me or reacted as though I was dirty. It was me who ignored them and turned away from them, because I judged myself lacking, and felt that I needed to compete with them in order to become visible. They were pretty and skinny, while I was fat and podgy. I obviously couldn't compete with them at that level, so I chose the only thing that they were unwilling to do, which was sex."*

On the issue of having affairs with married men:

> *"I am still competing with the pretty girl, and setting myself up for failure again and again. I truly do not want the affairs. I want my own husband and family but I pushed that desire deep down and ignored the voices inside of me that kept crying out for it. And because I don't have what I want, I become harsh and judgemental and critical of any woman who does."*

On the issue of growing up lonely:

> *"This process helped me to realise that my mother too, had spent her childhood alone. Gran was out all day trying to earn enough money just to keep head and shoulders above water for the two of them, after her husband died. When she became successful, she taught my mother to work hard for her success as well. As a single mother, my mom had to face the same issues, working hard to support herself and her daughter. All of us are very strong, capable women, but we all struggle with this crippling loneliness and inner emptiness, that work can't always fill."*

Escalating the strategy

The very real danger of maintaining a behavioural strategy that doesn't work any longer is that over time, the satisfaction achieved becomes less and less, and we need to escalate our behaviour simply to achieve the same level of satisfaction.

The woman who withdraws when feeling insecure, finds that in the beginning her partner is concerned and caring when she pulls away, and gives her the attention she craves. Over time, he becomes used to her 'silent treatment' and no longer gives the same level of concern when she withdraws into her shell, and so she no longer gets the same response of attention.

But this strategy has worked for her in the past, and so she needs to escalate it, in order to get the same level of attention, becoming even more depressed, morose, uncommunicative and silent.

The woman who screams at her partner for looking at another woman may find that it brings him in line to the way she wants him to behave in the beginning - but over time, as he realises that things are going to end up in an argument no matter what he does (damned if I do, damned if I don't), he stops jumping to attention when she starts to shout. The arguments and threats need to escalate, becoming more and more destructive before he gives in and does what she wants.

Like Sandra, who found that giving sex meant company which alleviated the loneliness for a time, only to find that the old strategy doesn't resolve her feelings of emptiness and loneliness for as long any more, and so escalates her behaviour to become more demanding of her lover and more critical and scathing of the time he spends with his family.

The solution is obvious when reading it in black and white. *If the strategy is no longer working, it is time to find a different strategy.* If the behaviour is no longer effective, then it's necessary to find an alternative, more appropriate behaviour that is effective in this situation.

What no longer works

What remains now is to stand back and take a good hard look at the coping strategies we put in place, and ask ourselves what deeper hidden need was met by this strategy. It is time to honestly assess which of those work well for us - and which have become redundant, out-dated and are no longer appropriate.

So where to from here?

Sandra's deep desires had become obscured by her coping
strategies:

1. I want friendships with men and women.

2. I want my own husband and children.

Figure 10: Desires versus Behaviours

Desire	Current Behaviour
I want friendships	I am bitchy to all women I meet, and always find some point to compare who they are with who I am. I need to prove to myself that I am better in some way. It doesn't make me any friends, that's for sure. In fact I am lonelier now than I was at school before everything started. After an in-depth dialogue with my inner voices, I realise that I made a very critical decision that I didn't want to be single like my mother and grandmother before me, which is why I made the decision to give sex for company. It's ironic that I discovered in this process, that my father was a married man who my mother had been involved for over 20 years. I didn't want to be like her, and yet I became exactly the same as her.
I want my own husband and children	I end up always with a married man, who has his own wife and children. He makes it very clear that this is just fun, he is not going to leave his wife and kids, and I always feel less than, the last choice. I know going in that the relationship has no possibility of a future, and yet I end up doing it again and again, I guess because I know how to play this role.

We can strengthen the possibility of that desire becoming a reality by focussing on what we want to manifest. If we can form a three dimensional mental image, almost like a mini-movie scene complete with sounds, feelings, intention, and visual tracks, we create more than a goal to work towards. The more intense we can make this movie scene, the stronger the feelings we can generate, the more the brain hooks into it as the future reality.

As the brain accepts that this is the future reality, our emotions and physiology absorb it as truth; this truth then starts to pulsate out into our energy field, and we find that we attract those aspects that are compatible with this future reality, and repel those that aren't.

Creating your future

Sandra, can you form an image of yourself about 8 months from now?

You are still successful in your job, and still busy, but there are some very interesting differences between you now, and you in the future.

The future you looks a little softer, and a little less tense. She is planning a dinner party with some friends for tonight; last night she went to a social gathering.

She has recently met a new man, who is available, and whose energy she enjoys immensely.

- Can you form an image of this possible you in the future

- Can you focus the picture so you can see what you look like in sharp detail?

Now, let's add to this picture. What sounds would you be hearing as you prepare for the dinner party in your apartment? What does your apartment look like as you set the dinner table, put flowers in the lounge? Do you hear vibrant jazzy music playing, or would the sounds be more soothing? Tune into the sounds that go with this energy for a while.

And let us add some more detail. What are you wearing right now? What are you planning to wear this evening? What does your face look like, your hair?

You are feeling good in this space. Not competitive, not needing to be powerful, but relaxed and calm, and that is showing on your face, in your shoulders. What is your body language like? Can you echo it now in this space? What is the energy and emotion within you in the future as you are preparing for this fun evening with new friends? Turn this emotion up, and feel this energy as it flows through your body.

Now, look around the room again. Everywhere you look, the colours seem to become more vibrant, the sounds more compelling, the feelings more intense.

Is there anything else you can add to make this future image more real?

When it as powerful and as vibrant as you can make it, take a step forward into this future you, and breathe deeply, as you inhabit the body, the mind, the emotions, of this you that you are willing to become.

Breathe deeply, as you take this reality deep into the core of you.

Feel it, really feel what it is like, to have friends, to have people who like your company, to have an available man interested in you for the very first time. Feel the joy of the possibility of a new relationship that for the first time, holds potential of a future.

Now, turn around and look back at the steps that you have taken over the past 8 months, to get to this point.

What did you do differently to attract friends into your space?

> *I became less critical, less vicious and sarcastic. I stopped waiting for someone to ask me for lunch, and asked if I could join them first. I apologised to my former secretary for being so bitchy, and sent her flowers when her baby was born. I joined the company's sport and social group. I joined the local chapter of a business woman's group*

What did you do differently to change the situation with married men?

> *I avoided married men! The minute I found out that they were married or even unavailable, I walked away, and said no thank you, and refused to get involved. In that way I sent a message out through my energy field that I was no longer available as a play thing, as a diversion on a boring business trip.*
>
> *In that way I also sent myself a powerful message that I am also worthy of a loving partner, not someone who simply is playing around, hurting his wife and me with his infidelity.*

Armed with concrete strategy of how to move from this stuck space of jealousy and non-relationship, Sandra was able to make definite, deliberate steps to claiming the power her future vision promised.

Key Points from this chapter

- ❖ Behind every action is a positive intention; the ensuing behaviour maybe destructive or negative, but the intention beneath it all, is positive. To change the negative behaviour we need to be willing to delve deep to find the positive intention beneath.

- ❖ Once we recognise the deeper intention, we can begin to explore more positive behaviours which can provide the desired result.

- ❖ We need to be honest with ourselves, to recognise whether our behavioural strategy is effective or no longer works. Escalating a strategy that is ineffective only entrenches us deeper into unhappiness and insecurity.

- ❖ Just as we hold within us all the voices and roles of our past, so too, we hold the voices, hopes and desires of our future selves. The power to create who we truly want to be exists within each and every one of us.

Self Reflection

1. Who do I need to forgive in order to let go of this unwanted emotion? Can I extend this same compassion and forgiveness to myself?

2. What are the positive intentions behind my behaviours? What is the inner voice truly trying to say through this negative or destructive behaviour?

3. If I critically examine my life, and the coping strategies I have put into place, if I am honest with myself …. Which ones no longer work, and need to be changed?

4. As I allow myself to form an image of myself in 8 months' time, at a time where I have done the work, and I am at a more successful place in my relationships with others and

with myself, what do I look like? Feel Like? Sound Like? Do I like that image and feel of the future me? How does it feel when I walk forward into that future me, and breathe the possibility of future in the here and now?

5. If I look back from that vantage point, what did I do specifically to make this future vision a reality?

I did this exercise when I was recovering from my divorce. In my future self, I had long dark hair (my hair was still quite short then), and it was flowing down my back. I was wearing a beautiful flowing white dress, and was walking through a summer garden filled with flowers toward a man who was waiting for me with love and acceptance and fidelity.

It was three years later that the vision became a very firm reality; Franz and I were looking at venues to hold our wedding. The venue we eventually chose had the most beautiful garden filled with flowers all year round. As I was walking through the garden towards Franz I had a powerful sense of déjàvu. My hair was long, I was wearing a soft white dress, and he was standing watching me, waiting for me to join him with such love and acceptance, that I had tears in my eyes as I reached his side.

I had, quite literally, created my future, three years before.

Chapter Ten:

Face to Face for the very first time

Up until now we have explored our conditioning and belief systems, had a look at our filters and coping decisions, discovered the various roles that we play in our everyday normal life, and listened to the voices that inhabit us. We've looked at current behaviour patterns and seen what link they have to previous experiences or conditioning.

Understanding our past, and reframing our experiences from a compassionate space of forgiveness is vital in changing our current behaviour. Honouring the hopes and dreams of our future possibilities is essential in creating our future reality.

Now we examine the current event and experience, and discuss coping strategies and new belief systems that are reflective of this change in thinking.

In Chapter Four, we spoke briefly about how any current event needed three factors in order to survive: *Seeds, Soil, Sustenance.*

We have seen how we provide both fertile *soil* (our belief system set in place by our previous experiences) and the *sustenance* (negative self-talk, or self-image, lack of worth, value that nourishes the seeds and allows the plant to grow and flourish).

There also have to be *seeds:* A comment, a current feeling of insecurity, an action that seems incongruent with what we believe the correct behaviour to be. The seeds are the external trigger from our partner, or from a situation, and so for the first time in this book so far, we turn to what is happening in your life right now. The seeds, or in other words, the event or episode happening *right now* that is causing you distress and tension sufficient to trigger a jealous or insecure reaction.

Sometimes that is all that is required to collapse the negative behaviour is that we have an understanding of our behaviour and how it came into being in the first place. What is more often the case, however, is that with the understanding also comes the need to learn a new behaviour. We need to learn a new song with different dance steps as it were, so that we do not automatically default into what is a well-rehearsed and comfortable movement, simply because we have danced that way for so many years.

Becoming a witness to our behaviour

The first step to diffusing any emotion that is building up in response to a current trigger or environment is to become aware of your body, your breathing and how you feel when you are relaxed. In this way, you are then able to become aware of how that changes as soon as you become tense, agitated and responding with jealousy or insecurity.

Our body registers our distress long before our brain catches up and makes a decision on how to speak or act.

Anna said that when she stopped to become aware of how her body was responding in instances when she became jealous or sensitive, (like when a pretty waitress was serving them, or they bumped into one of his female colleagues from the office), that she noticed that her breathing became very shallow, she started to get prickles of heat stabbing in her scalp and temples, and her throat felt as though it was constricted and tight.

"I had had no awareness that my body registered my panic this way, before I had even said a word," she said in amazement.

"Now when I get that feeling of prickles of heat in my head, I stop and breathe, and ask myself what is around me that is threatening, or a reminder of a previous experience in my childhood."

When Sandra did this she became aware of a tight, jagged feeling in her stomach, and a rigid clamp forcing her shoulders into an uncomfortable position. As she hunched over with the "weight" in her shoulders, and trying to shield her stomach from her jagged pain, her face became brittle and harsh. She suddenly caught a glimpse of herself in the mirror, and was stunned by how accusatory and vicious she looked.

"No wonder women are so intimidated by me" she said, "if I look like that. No wonder men go running back to their soft gentle welcoming wives and they don't want to stay with me."

Think of way your body responds, as your physical clue to pay attention to what is happening, within you and around you.

As you witness and observe the way your body responds to a stimulus, you give yourself time to:

- Breathe with compassion into those parts of your body that are responding with distress.

- Objectively look at the situation and assess whether it is frightening and threatening, or is this simply a reminder of a past experience that still needs attention and more healing.

- If it is a past experience you can adapt your behaviour accordingly: as in, there is nothing to be frightened of in this moment, and as soon as I have time, I will honour this distress and pay it the attention that it needs, and validate and heal these feelings

- If it is a current experience that is threatening you, as a witness, you become AWARE of your actions and statements, not simply blindly regurgitating a previous programme.

- As you act with awareness and consciousness, and responsibility for your actions and words, you move from a space of being a victim of the situation. Instead you become consciously cognisant of it, which is an entirely different emotional response.

What is true

This allows you to ask yourself if the distress your body is registering is because there is a *real threat*, or whether it is simply your *filters* that are at work, shaping the landscape to what we perceive it to be, not what it truly is.

Each time you feel threatened; ask yourself whether the threat is real? Is it really one hundred percent, totally, absolutely, real?

Is it possible that what I am responding to is not real? Would it change the way I think, behave, act, speak, if this was not real at this time?

Of course it would.

If Anna thinks that Stefan is longing to flirt with the waitress, but is not doing because he's scared of the fight that will ensue, she is already,

a) suspicious

b) angry

c) on high alert, showing significant amounts of body distress

Meanwhile, the truth is, nothing has happened at all!

Stefan hasn't flirted with the waitress, in actual fact he has barely even noticed her. By assuming that he is itching to flirt with the waitress and would so much rather Anna was not even around, it sets the seeds for an explosive argument to take place. How much more different would the conversation and emotion be if we stopped, just for a moment to ask what is *really* true?

Until we know that something is true, we cannot accuse our partner of something that we feel, or even because of our body distress. What if it's not true? What if Anna could believe that Stefan is not longing to flirt with the waitress, but in actual fact is so enjoying flirting with his beautiful girlfriend.

Would that change the way she behaved during lunch! You bet.

Separate fact from fantasy

The mind is an exceptionally powerful thing, able of conjuring up thoughts, images, visions of both delight and torture. At the slightest provocation, our minds can provide a fully enlivened screenplay in our heads, complete with sound, words, and a music track to boot.

We are capable of imagining details and embellishing events, colouring them out of all perspective from reality, so they no longer bear even a passing semblance to the initial event.

As we imagine scenes and words that we have no way of even knowing if they ever happened that way or not, the emotions get involved. As we picture our partner in a passionate clinch or some intimate encounter, our stomach clenches and knots, we feel nauseous, the blood drains from our head and we end up having a full on physical reaction *to an event that has only happened in our heads.*

When he tells you that he has to work late, and your mind supplies the secretary planning an intimate dinner for two underneath the desk; or she says that she had a glass of champagne at work to celebrate the department meeting targets at the end of the month, and your mind conjures up a long boozy lunch with that smarmy sales guy who has joined her company ... Recognise that you are dealing with fantasy.

> **Fact:** She had something to drink, she told you, and you can smell it on her breath when you kiss her hello as she gets in the car.

> **Fantasy:** anything else your mind tells you happened, *because you do not know this to be true.*

Or perhaps:

> **Fact:** He will be home late because he has told you he has to work.

> **Fantasy:** His secretary is also staying with him, and is rubbing his shoulders even while he is speaking to you.

The minute you find yourself descending into fantasy, bring your thinking back to what you know to be true. Write it down if you have to, so that it is staring at you in black and white.

Say it to yourself while you are looking in the mirror, so you can hear yourself verbally speaking what you do know to be true.

For instance, if your partner has just phoned to say he will unexpectedly be working late tonight, you could do the following:

Logically assess the facts as you know them

- He is working late tonight, he said he will phone me when he knows what time he will be coming home.

- He will either get something to eat at work, or he will be starving when he comes home.

- When he comes home, he will have worked 4 or 5 hours longer than normal, and so he will probably be exhausted.

- If he is tired, he will be uncommunicative and not wish to have a long conversation about his day or what he was up to or even who else was working with him. I know I wouldn't if it were me in his place.

Then make an appropriate behaviour decision

- I will carry on with my normal routine for the evening, and will wait for his call. He said he will call, and so I will wait for that call, not keep contacting him every 30 minutes wanting to know the details.

- I will fill my time with activities that fulfil me, and validate me. I am able to enjoy my own time in a self-productive way, without my partner by my side.

- Unless he tells me otherwise, I will assume that he will still want supper when he comes home, and so I will cook as normal and keep his food for him.

- If he is tired when he comes home, and doesn't want to eat, or talk to me, I will assume that it is because he has worked hard and had a very long day (logical response) and not because he doesn't want to talk to me or spend time with me (emotionally insecure response). I will let him recover from this event in a calm supportive environment, as I would want him to do for me when I have to work late.

If the mind creates a fantasy

- Follow the feeling, and ask yourself, what am I feeling right now?

- What is the inner voice inside me saying right now

- If I recognise that this voice is trying to protect me, what emotion or feeling does this voice represent?

- Can I remember a time before when I felt this way?

- What does this voice need from me, what does this part of me need from me, right now, in order to feel better and secure with my partner working late?

- How would I normally behave when I heard this kind of news?

- Does it work for me? My partner?

- What other coping strategies could I employ that would change the outcome for both of us in a positive manner?

- What are three positive things that I can do for me right now that will change the way I would normally respond to this feeling?

When we work from fantasy, we put entire coping strategies into play that are simply not appropriate, because they come from a point of conjecture and imagination, not from a place of reality.

We enter into punishing routines with our partner when they don't even deserve to be 'punished' - because of something that happened entirely in our heads.

If you fly off the handle because she had a glass of champagne at the office meeting, you are punishing her for what you think happened - the long boozy lunch, instead of the innocent glass in the office meeting to celebrate meeting targets. (Other facts will tell you whether she has been drinking all afternoon, or not. If you know she giggles after one glass of champagne, that is not evidence to imagine an afternoon at the pub.)

Rick had fallen head over heels for a young divorcee, with two young sons. She had made it very clear to him when they met that she was not ready to settle down again quickly. A teen bride, and divorced at 29, Sophia wanted to have the fun time she felt she had missed out as a young girl.

They had been dating informally for about three months when she told him that she and four of her girlfriends had booked a ladies only cruise to celebrate her 30th birthday. "My stomach clenched into knots when I realised that she would be going without me. I knew what fun people get up to on a ship and I was sick with jealousy that she would be getting into bed with a different guy every night."

Rick's mind wreaked absolute havoc with him for the five days that she was away, and he was sickened by the nightly movie that would play in his head, as he imagined her having all sorts of fun without him.

By the time Sophia got back, tanned and relaxed, with presents for him from her vacation, he was seething with resentment and anger. She had come back ready for a relationship with him; he punished her repeatedly with arguments and intense questioning about what she had got up to on the ship.

They broke up soon afterwards, because of the imagined infidelities he had 'seen' her enjoy each night she was away.

Said Sophia sadly, "The ironic thing in all of this is that we had so much fun together as ladies, and really let our hair down – but except for the expected flirty chatting with guys on board, there was none of the raucous behaviour Rick was convinced I had got up to. I just couldn't make him see sense, he was so hooked onto what he believed to be true."

Sticking to what is, separating fact from fantasy is the first weapon in your arsenal for diffusing the sting out of a current trigger.

Keep your thinking time appropriate

The only time that you have a right to claim is the time you have spent together in a committed relationship. Not what happened before, and not what comes afterwards.

Your partner had a life before he met you, a life that included parents and family events, schooling, university or educational events, friends and social events, and lovers, girlfriends, maybe even a fiancée or a wife. He had life experiences that did not include you.

Yet for so many people, coming to terms with their partner's past is incredibly difficult. Accepting that he loved someone else and enjoyed someone else's company the way he enjoys yours right now, riles some people up towards jealousy and insecurity.

I did it myself. I was so convinced that he had a whale of a time in his relationship before me, that I forgot that he was obviously having an even better time with me, *otherwise he would not have stayed with me.*

It feels like a betrayal somehow, to think that he loved someone else, and we end up wounding ourselves again and again by fantasizing that what went before was by far better than what he has right now.

And yet it is critical to remember that:

- He had a past life before he met you, and all of this is in his past.

- If it helps, draw a time line of your partner's life, and chart where you entered into his life. It gives a visual reminder that he lived for many years before he even met you.

- It cannot ever be seen as a betrayal of you and your relationship because (fact) he didn't even know that you existed at the time.

- He is the man he is precisely because of his life's experiences, understandings and journey, and that is what attracted you to him.

- It is a good thing that he has had intimate experiences before you, because it has helped him to understand what he is looking for in a long term partner. (And face it, dating a forty-something year old man who has never even kissed a girl before would be just a little bit weird!).

- If his past life had been as fantastic as you imagine it to be, *he would still be there with that person.* He would have settled down, and got married and had a life and children if things had been that wonderful. The fact that he didn't tells you that the reality of his past relationships was not as fulfilling and glorious as you are convincing yourself it was.

You also need to remember, that, like him, YOU also had a past life before meeting him, before finding out that he existed, and your past life experiences, good and bad, have helped to shape who you are today.

Your past life doesn't betray your love for him in any way does it? So why should his?

It was before your time. As simple as that.

Louise is not worried about the past, she is able to accept that her current partner had a marriage and children before he met her. But she seethes with resentment that her ex-husband is now having the time of his life with his new girlfriend.

They are always going away on weekends and trips, and get to stay in lovely guest lodges and hotels, and when he took her to France on a business-cum-vacation trip, she became incandescently angry.

"He never did anything like that with me," she fumed. "We had to sponge off friends and family if we ever went away – which of course was not very often because he worked all hours that God sent."

Keep your thinking realistic. When Louise and Alan met, they were both very young. Alan was a young inexperienced legal assistant struggling to finish his final exams and hold down a very busy job at the same time. There was no money then, and every available moment was spent studying or working towards a future goal. Now, 11 years later, he is a qualified attorney, earning far more money, and now that he is not spending all his spare time on studying, he has both more time and more money on his hands. It is unrealistic to compare what he was capable of 11 years prior, to now. Of course his earning capacity has increased through the years.

This has got nothing to do with whether you were worth it or not (that is your negative self-talk, not his). It has to do simply with being a little older, a little more well off, and a little more time to enjoy it now.

What he does now with his relationships is out of your time zone. You can only claim the time that the two of you spent together in a committed relationship, you cannot claim ownership of his future relationships. The marriage is over, and his responsibility and commitment to you ended with the divorce decree.

The issue here is letting go of him and releasing him, not viewing his subsequent relationships as a continued betrayal of you.

Agree on the relationship boundaries

You have decided that it's time to make your dating a little more formal, and to make a commitment of sorts. It doesn't have to end up in an engagement ring or marriage or even the key to the front door, it might be something as simple as 'we have got something good happening here, I'd like to make this an exclusive relationship, so that I know you are my girlfriend, and not seeing any other men, and vice versa for you.'

This is the time to agree the relationship boundaries with mutual agreement on issues that work for both of you.

Some issues to consider:

- Living our own lives: we may be in a committed relationship together, but to what extent are we comfortable with each other's individual activities. If he plays county cricket during summer and league action cricket in winter, he is not going to be happy if his girlfriend insists that he spends every evening and weekend with her. If she is a member of the champion team at the pub quiz on a Wednesday night, she will not be thrilled if he turns around and says that now must be forfeit if we are in a committed relationship together.

- Friends of the opposite sex: I know one couple who have made all their friends joint friends, and that they do all their socialising together. They wouldn't dream of meeting a friend of the opposite sex without their partner being along as well. For another, both partners are comfortable with the fact that his best friend is a girl he was at school with, and that he calls her once a week for a catch up chat, and meets her regularly for lunch. For another, she runs a business with her ex-husband, and discovered that they are ideal business partners whereas they made a lousy couple. What works for you? What would you honestly feel comfortable with? This is the time to discuss it at the outset, not seethe about it for 8 months before exploding and delivering an ultimatum.

It doesn't have to be heavy handed, e.g.: 'no talking to members of the opposite sex' – that is likely to scare away even the most ardent of suitors.

But it can be reflective of what you really need to clarify as you move into a relationship, for instance. "Trust and faith for me are vital in a relationship, and I believe it is important that we can trust each other to behave in a manner that is respectful towards each other."

It's ironic isn't it that we have no problem in declaring our sexual status, "Before we have unprotected sex, can we just confirm our HIV status?" or "I am AIDS and STD's free, I had my last test after my marriage dissolved and I am all clear." Yet we struggle with the really critical statement of "Before I allow myself to fall deeply in love with you, I need to know that you will hold my heart gently and treat me and this relationship respectfully."

When agreeing your relationship parameters, be honest with yourself. If an issue makes you uncomfortable, allow yourself to explore what is happening inside you, what emotions are trying to speak out. If you feel uncomfortable that she works with her ex-husband, for example, explore why that particular issue is a hot spot for you, and makes you feel insecure.

It is an opportunity for healing an old wound. Yes it's uncomfortable, but the relief it will provide as your relationship continues to grow and she continues to work with her ex-husband will be immense.

Honour your partner's needs

When Rick became jealous and insecure about Sophia planning a single's birthday cruise, he was thinking of his needs and wants, "I want her to be with me exclusively."

What he was not cognisant of, he later realised, was her needs at the time. She had just ended a long term relationship and had told him that she was not ready for another serious commitment straight away. She had planned her 30th birthday cruise for years before she had even met him, (since her 21st birthday) and had long dreamed of this ladies only excursion. She had felt stifled in her marriage for years, and needed to let her hair down, and rediscover the fun and joy that life had to offer without needing it to come packaged with a lover.

She needed to reconnect with herself and time in which to do it. He wanted to keep her by his side, and his insecurity made him need to control her.

In any relationship there needs to be an ebbing and flowing, a recognising and meeting of each other's needs. There are times that one partner will seem to give more, and the other take. As the natural energy of the relationship expands and flows, this give and take should also flow so that each partner is giving and receiving what is needed at the time.

Step back and look at what your partner is truly trying to say about what they need. Ask them to explain to you what it is they need at this point in time, from the relationship, from you, from this phase of their life, and then repeat it back to them with the words: "Let me see if I understand this; you are saying ..."

Write it down, so that you can see the flow and logic of it represented before you. And then stand back from the situation and examine your needs, and see whether what your partner is asking for is reasonable and do-able.

Rick regrets the way he handled Sophia's cruise plans. "We had been dating for only three months, and were by no means a committed item yet, because she was just not ready to commit to anything more serious or long-term than plans for the following weekend.

"I knew she needed space and time, and yet I kept pushing her for more. I should have realised that if she was resisting getting into something heavy with me, she would most certainly be the same with anybody else, yet all I heard was that she wasn't ready for a long term relationship *with me*, and I felt completely rejected by her."

Understand your needs

If you have worked through the previous chapters, you will have discovered what it is that you need in relationship in order to feel safe, and also, what are your trigger points for insecurity and jealousy.

If like Sandra, your need is for someone special and intimate to share your life, then make a decision about the one night stands, or getting involved with somebody who is married and therefore unavailable, before it happens. That way, if you find out during a flirty session at the pool bar that he is married, you can cross this one mentally off your internal check list. *'He is married, and I need someone who is available, so therefore I will not let this go any further.'* Just the verbal statement of this realisation is a powerful reminder that you are worth more from a relationship.

Monique has just made a similar decision in her life. A career woman, she travels extensively, and just doesn't seem to have the time to find and sustain long term relationships, and so has entered into a number of 'friends with benefits' arrangements across the planet. It seemed to work for a while, until she found herself falling in love with a Dutch 'friend'.

"Suddenly I didn't want to have 'benefits' with anyone else, I wanted to be with him. Things had moved from great sex to feeling like I was making love with him, and I felt almost as though I was being unfaithful to him when I was with a 'friend' while I was working in Atlanta," she said.

She plucked up the courage to tell him that she had discovered she wanted more out of their arrangement. She wanted a relationship with him. He on the other hand was not interested in anything more serious – he also travelled the world, he also had similar arrangements with other female friends, and was not ready to settle for just one steady girlfriend in his life.

Monique was forced to decide. Was she willing to continue the arrangement with him, or did she want more? She decided to end it with him and not see him again, because she couldn't bear the thought of just being one of his girls. "I wanted intimacy, commitment, a relationship, and that's what I was ready for. What we wanted had changed and was no longer compatible - but I recognised that *my* needs had changed, not his."

Ironically this story has a happy ending. When he realised that she was serious, and would rather no longer see him at all, he began to miss her presence. They had been 'together' for over a year, and he had enjoyed her being in his life far more than he had thought.

Gradually, his other friendships began to lose their appeal, as he felt her absence more and more keenly.

Six months later she opened her front door to find him standing there with a huge bunch of burnt orange roses, asking whether she would consider being his one and only girlfriend. He would rather have her in his life completely, than not at all.

Hear what is really being said

It is something we are all guilty of at one time or another. Our partner says one thing and we hear another thing entirely.

The other day I was feeling particularly out of shape after our long hard winter (not enough gym, and too many cups of hot chocolate), and was examining myself critically in the mirror as I was getting dressed. My husband walked into the bedroom, and pulled open the curtains and said, "Spring is on the way! You'll be able to go back to gym soon!"

He was linking the fact that it was spring with the fact that I do not like to drive on icy, snowy roads, which is the main reason I do not get to gym in winter. Now the snow had melted, I could go back to gym each day.

I, however, linked it to that I was looking as much out of shape as I felt, and definitely not ready for spring. I thought he was saying: "if you don't like what you see in the mirror you better start exercising again."

I snapped at him, and could feel myself beginning to get annoyed. I mean, he doesn't go to gym at all, how dare he criticise me?

He took one look at my face and said: "Oh no, what did I say?" That simple sentence stopped me in my tracks. What exactly did he say? He said the spring was coming back and that I could go back to gym soon.

What did I hear? That I was out of shape, heading rapidly towards clinically obese because I had gorged myself on hot chocolate and delicious German pastries all winter, and should not even think of putting on a swimming costume any time soon.

Our relationships are full of these miscommunications, and feelings that get hurt because of what we thought was said, instead of what really was said.

Before you allow yourself to get upset or hurt, stop and regurgitate exactly what was said. You supplied the feelings and the interpretation, not your partner. Ask for clarification if you think you've misunderstood what was said, as in:

"What I think you just said was ... did I hear you correctly?"

When Rick responded to Sophia's plan to go on a cruise, he didn't hear that she had planned this event and dreamed of it for the last 9 years, which was what was said. He only heard that she didn't want to spend her 30th birthday with him, which is information that was not said *but that he supplied.* He crucified himself with feelings of inadequacy and rejection, when if he had stopped to hear and reflect on what was really being said, he could have saved himself an enormous amount of hurt.

Is it any of your business really?

The two of you have ended a relationship, and a couple of months later you find out that she is now dating one of your good friends. Or that her new boyfriend is helping her to renovate her house, and she has bashed down the front wall that you thought was one of the best features of the garden.

You discover a box of old love letters from his ex-girlfriend when you help him move house.

Or the fact that he still plays tennis with her brother every month.

You hear via a friend that your ex-husband is planning to go and work on contract overseas for a few years, or that he has just invested in his new girlfriend's business.

And before it hits you like a punch in the stomach, take a deep breath and ask yourself very critically: "Is this anything to do with me?"

Is this any of my business what he is doing now with his new girlfriend, with his money? Is it anything to do with me that she has started renovating her new home and is knocking down what I repeatedly told her was a valuable feature of the house? These love letters are old and written way before my time. Does it have anything to do with me at all?

And if the answer is NO, it really doesn't, then follow the emotion and the wounding that is screaming through you, and listen to what is happening inside your body and mind. Go back to point 1, (is it fact or fantasy) to make sure you are dealing with what *is*, not what you think *might be*.

- Follow the feeling, and ask yourself, what am I feeling right now?

- What is the inner voice inside me saying right now?

- If I recognise that this voice is trying to protect me, what emotion or feeling does this voice represent?

- Can I remember a time before when I felt this way?

- What does this voice need from me, what does this part of me need from me, right now, in order to feel better and secure with this information?

- What behavioural strategy can I adopt right now that allows my inner voice to be validated in this situation.

When the ex just won't go away

There are times in a relationship when you realise that too many people are involved.

When his ex-girlfriend keeps interfering, or her ex-husband just won't go away, you need to make some decisions together as a couple.

- Ask yourself whether the ex really is interfering, or is this simply a deeper insecurity flaring up. If this truly is a case of interfering, you will have concrete facts to point to as opposed to a nebulous feeling of unease.

- Be honest with your partner, that you are feeling uncomfortable with the amount of head space and emotional energy the ex has in your new relationship, and point to the facts to support your observations, not the emotion. If he has run a business with his ex for years, and now the disintegration of the relationship means that they have to settle business issues, or sell property, recognise it as a move toward closure for both of them and give it time. That's a very different issue to finding her following you as you drive down the coast for a day's outing, only to meet her sitting at the lunch table next to you, or her sending him an intimate and inappropriate Christmas present when you have been in a relationship for nearly a year.

- Decide what is important to you as a couple, (honesty, fidelity, trust, feeling comfortable with each other in all situations) and decide on what is the priority of this relationship

- Once you have a priority for the relationship – e.g.: to honour each other and ourselves, you can develop the game plan together. A united front is necessary for showing the ex that their time is over and so, his or her continued involvement is no longer appropriate in your relationship. Make sure that you are sending the same message – e.g.: this is a committed relationship and we are faithful to each other.

- Explore your own issues of trust / inadequacy / comparisons that come up for you, and see where they originated. This represents an opportunity to heal old wounds as well.

- Keep yourself focussed on the current relationship, and do not get sucked into what they used to do when they were together. Your relationship has a completely different dynamic and cannot be compared to anything else, because of this.

When Maria and Ted got married, his ex-girlfriend, Helena became exceptionally persistent; 'manipulative might be a better word,' says Maria. She knew what time he finished work, and would phone him in tears, asking for help over things that he used to do when he lived with her: changing light-bulbs, moving garden refuse, hanging up a new curtain rail, cleaning the pool filter.

She used to put on this little girl lost act that drove me insane - "I would if I knew how, but Ted, you always did that kind of thing around the house, and now that you have gone, I don't know how to do it myself"- and Ted would just fall for it every time. When we argued over it, he would ask me what choice did he have? He couldn't just leave her in tears to struggle when she was taking more time than he had to recover from their breakup and move on with her life.

(More time in this instance being over two and a half years).

We finally reached resolution when we both stepped back from the issue and re-examined our relationship priorities and discussed what qualities where important in each of us to achieve that priority.

When she would phone, he would listen to what she wanted, and if it wasn't an absolute emergency, he would say that he was sorry that he was busy and so couldn't help this time, could she call her brother or father to help her. If she phoned the home phone, I would answer, saying no, he couldn't come to the phone, he was busy, and was it an emergency, in which case he would help of course, but otherwise could she call a friend or neighbour to help. We didn't avoid her or ignore her. We made sure that she was safe and unharmed (which Ted needed to know), but we kept deferring her to a more appropriate person to help her.

We presented a united front to her and it took a while, but eventually she got the message and went away.

When the rest of family is involved

Tracey recently became engaged to Tony, a divorced father of two teenage girls, aged 17 and 15, and is very happy with him except for one thing.

"His family are still very involved with his ex-wife; she spends holidays with them, and even came round for Boxing Day with the girls to celebrate with them all. They still talk about her as if she was part of the family, and then when they realise I am there now, they become really embarrassed."

It's important to remember in a case like this that she does have a legitimate relationship with his family. She is the mother of their grandchildren, was a member of their family for nearly 15 years, and they have built up a relationship with each other over that time.

Whenever a marriage disintegrates, it's not just two people who are affected. It is the children, the family, the grandparents, the aunts and uncles who also need time to achieve closure and resolution with the fact that the marriage has ended.

However, as your relationship becomes more serious, it is the responsibility of your partner to ensure an appropriate weaning off the ex-partner within his family, by making his wishes and feelings known to his family. Give it time. The ex became part of the family over time, and it will take time to wean them off, especially if they have grown fond of each other during the marriage.

For second wives and husbands, you must understand that there will be times when you can expect (and therefore must be prepared) to have the ex-partner included in the family gathering.

The children's birthdays and birthday parties, parents evenings at the school, prize-giving and sports days when they are young, through to engagements, weddings and new babies as they grow older, are events and rites of passage that belong to *both* parents, and to their extended families. However, you do have the right to expect that the family's loyalty will be with their son or daughter and the new partner, at these gatherings.

It's harsh but true to remember that what they feel for each other happened before your time, and really has nothing to do with you. They know the ex very well, through many years of getting to know each other. It belonged to another time zone, before your time. It doesn't take away from what they will come to feel for you as you become a more permanent part of their family.

Remember Louise and Alan? One of Louise's biggest grievances was that the new girlfriend has 'taken my place with my ex in-laws.'

"I worked so hard to make that relationship good and strong, and I really thought they loved me and accepted me as part of the family. To find that they are able to just dump me and switch their loyalty to the new girlfriend is galling. I am so angry with them, with Alan, with the new girlfriend. It's as if she has just stepped into my life and taken it over."

It's after your time. Beyond your timeframe, and you have no claim on any relationship they form with the new girlfriend after your marriage has ended.

Harsh words. But critical to acknowledge and accept in order to move forward, and not be disabled any longer. You don't have to like it. You do, however, have to acknowledge that this is the way it is.

When children are involved

Children add an entirely different dynamic to a relationship, and it is normal these days to find family units of your kids/ my kids/ our kids. Step parenting is an entire other subject, another book, (indeed, another series of books) because it entails dealing with so many complex issues: the emotional debris of a broken home, creating a safe space for the children to heal and regain their equilibrium, merging of children from different families into a new unit with step-siblings, new parents or authority figures, changing of routines, homes, as they have to get used to a new 'normal'.

It is an issue that cannot be dealt with here in a few paragraphs or even a few chapters: There are many excellent programmes, often state run social welfare projects, available to help negotiate this difficult terrain as two family units become one, and they are worth while exploring.

Key Points of this chapter

❖ The current event that is happening is simply a trigger, a reflection of a deeper insecurity, and needs to be explored.

❖ There are positive behavioural strategies to employ in overcoming the moment, before I can do the deeper internal work.

❖ I need to first witness and be aware of what is happening in the here and now so that I can make an appropriate behaviour and coping decision.

Self reflection

1. How does my body respond to a perceived trigger? What are some of my physical signs that my body is picking up a threat or stimulus?

2. Is the threat real? Is it 100 % really, really true.

3. How would my behaviour change if I believed it was not true?

4. What do I need to do to honour myself within this relationship?

5. How can I honour my partner's needs without compromising my own

6. What are the priorities of our relationship? For me? For my partner?

Chapter Eleven:

When the Monster Bites Back

You are updating your face book site, and you suddenly realise that your husband has added a new friend to his friendship board - his old flame from University, the one who was gorgeous, and smart, with long red hair down to her knees. She has added a post to his wall saying that a group of them are getting together on Friday afternoon for a drink and she would love to catch up with him again.

Your wife receives an invitation to join the committee for the tennis club's Christmas bash, and you know the chairman has a crush on her. If she joins the committee she will be with him every Wednesday night from now until Christmas, and you just know he is going to make a play for her at every opportunity.

You are attending your fiancée's company summer beach bash, when you become aware that she is spending an enormous amount of time with the new sales guy who has just transferred in from another branch.

What do you do? Is something happening? Does that old adage, 'where there's smoke there's fire' hold any water? Or are you just being silly and over-reacting?

Is it really something to worry about?

No matter what situation you are faced with, you can buy yourself time before you respond, by paying attention to what is going on inside of you. Only then is it time to look at what is happening around you, in the current situation and with your partner.

Breathe slowly and rhythmically, taking your breath deep down to the base of your spine, holding it there for a second and then breathing out slowly. Take the breath directly in to the part of your body that holds this feeling of unease or confusion, and just focus on breathing into that space for a moment or two.

Then, drink a glass of water, go for a walk in the garden, and bring your physical response back to normal.

Try to pinpoint exactly what it is that is worrying you? That he will meet his ex-flame on Friday night for a drink, and compare how well she has aged over the years next to you? Or whether he made the right decision in marrying you instead of her? Or that her intentions are not honourable? Or maybe there is a fear that he has become bored with the comfortable familiar routine that has been established over the past few years? Or are you worried that he hadn't told you about it before you discovered it on Facebook?

Follow the emotion inside of you and reflect on:

- Is the way I am responding due to what is happening right now or does it come from a deeper level of anxiety or concern.

- When was the last time I felt this way?

- Am I being factual?

- Am I hearing what has been said?

- Am I responding to something before or after my time?

- Does this current situation honour the relationship?

- Has this kind of situation made me uneasy before in my relationship or is this an isolated case.

- Does it honour both me and my partner?

- Is it really anything to do with me; is it my business right now?

- Is the way I am about to respond going to honour the relationship/ me/ my partner.

Then you are more able to respond from a space of personal power, where you are acting with self-integrity and awareness, instead of *reacting* to either the situation, a person, or an old wounding.

You have the right to express unease if you see a situation that you feel does not honour the relationship, but make sure that you are seeing it for what it is. (And in order to do this, make sure you are separating the fact from the fantasy).

- Is your fiancée flirting outrageously with the new sales guy sending out signals of availability and interest, or did she simply end up standing next to him when they selected volleyball teams, and is now laughing at all of his jokes?

- Did your husband specifically not tell you he was meeting his ex-girlfriend for a drink, or has life been so hectic and crazy over the past few days that he hasn't had chance?

- You're eating yourself up that your wife is spending time with the tennis chairman, because you know he likes her. Does she reciprocate those feelings, or does she simply put up with his advances and flirty comments because she really enjoys working on the committee?

Bring your fear or unease into the light and discuss it from your centre of self-respect and integrity.

> "I must confess I felt a slight twinge when I heard that you are going to meet Vanessa for a drink on Friday. I know that I have nothing to worry about, because you and I have a wonderful solid relationship, but I felt a little uneasy about it."

as opposed to a space of insecurity and vulnerability

> "How long have you been seeing her? Do you still love her? Why are you going to see her anyway, she's old history, do you still think about her? Do you wish you had married her? I don't want you to go. If you loved me, you wouldn't go."

The former approach indicates acceptance that it is your emotional response not his untrustworthiness that is the issue, and conveys no blame or accusation, simply acknowledgement of how you feel. If you have a history of honouring each other and the relationship, then you know that you can probably trust him to continue behaving in that fashion.

The latter approach screams vulnerability, insecurity, manipulation and control: 'if you love me you won't do anything that makes me feel uncomfortable or uneasy'. Of course as we have learned throughout this book, is that there will always be a trigger for that insecurity and vulnerability, and if it's not meeting the ex-girlfriend, something else will surely surface.

When there really is a fire

For years Sam had watched her husband Greg flirting with her brother's wife. They were good friends, and whenever there was a family gathering, the two of them would always be at the centre of the fun. "My brother Rob is a pilot and is often away, and so it became natural for Greg to pop around and see if Annie needed anything during those times. I kept telling myself that it was just what families do, looking after each other, and that I was silly to be jealous and insecure. And yet I couldn't shake this feeling of unease if they ever spent time alone together," said Sam.

The crux came when Rob returned home unexpectedly. There had been an airline strike, and his flight was cancelled that day. He came home a few hours later, to find his wife and his brother in law in bed together. "He came round to my office and told me to take the rest of the day off, and then took me home to confront them both."

"We both lost our marriages that day. Cornered, they brazened things out and decided that they were going to move in together, and Rob and I could sort out the kids between us.

"After they had left together, Rob poured us both a stiff drink and told me that he had always suspected that something was going on, but had ignored his gut instinct, thinking that Greg would never do that to me. We had both known, yet had both tried to ignore those deeper clues and feelings."

Julie had been married to Darren for many years, and had often felt that he was playing around. "I'd had a shocking childhood, which left me vulnerable and deeply insecure. Each time I felt that he was attracted to someone else I would react badly, questioning and interrogating and checking up on him.

"He told me that I was jealous, paranoid and insecure, and that I needed help, and of course, because I so desperately wanted to believe that he wasn't playing around, I chose to believe that I was the one who was damaged.

"I ended up going to a psychiatrist begging for treatment for my paranoia and jealousy, as obviously I had a serious problem. I spent years on anti-depressants and tranquilisers, believing that I needed them to keep me sane.

"I had been married about 20 years when it all came tumbling out that he had been cheating on me since before we were married, and had had many liaisons and even a couple of long term affairs during our marriage.

"Instead of being shattered as I always thought I would be, I was so angry. I had been under psychiatric treatment for almost 8 years, because of my insane jealousy and insecurity, and now he was telling me that I was NOT insane, that I had every right to be jealous, because he was playing all over town.

"I was so angry that nearly everyone knew as well, but hadn't told me. He had made me keep the fact that I was on medication (and for what) a secret. I could quite easily have killed him at that point.

"He wanted to try to save the marriage. I had possibly one of the sanest moments of my life as I had envisioned life with him at 50, 60 and beyond into 70 and even 80. He wouldn't change, he would still play all over town, and I just couldn't bear to spend another day with him as his wife."

Eric had always felt a little bit intimidated by his wife's boss. He was charming and smooth and incredibly good looking, and she was his PA, which meant she spent an enormous amount of time working exclusively with him. When they started travelling around the country to visit all the branches and distributors, I was panicked. I imagined long evenings together, sharing bottles of wine over intimate dinners for two.

I kept telling myself that I was being ridiculous – she had a job she liked, a great working relationship with her boss and enjoyed the company she worked for. It was only when she starting taking more interest in her appearance that I began to worry seriously; she had never been one for painting her nails or wearing make-up during the day, and now suddenly she was going off on shopping sprees for snazzy new business suits, having her hair restyled and her nails done, and wearing mascara and lipstick.

I confronted her, and of course she denied it, saying she just was trying to look her best because she was now working with executive directors and needed to look the part. I let it ride for months, biting back my feelings of jealousy and fear, each time she had to work late, or over a weekend, or went off on a business trip.

Eventually I got a phone call from her boss's wife. She had seen them together having a very intimate lunch. She had suspected that something had been going on for months and so had followed her husband when he said that he had to work through the weekend for the umpteenth time.

I felt like I had been kicked in the stomach by a horse. I had thought it was happening but that was nothing compared to the feeling of actually having it confirmed.

Discovering that your worst fears are true and that your partner is having an affair is the worst type of betrayal. You have made a public commitment to each other, if not one of marriage then certainly one that has 'announced' you as a couple to your friends and community, and so it is an absolute betrayal of that public intention to be in a committed partnership. It also means that you have been lied to, as your partner has made up excuses and stories to cover the truth, an issue that many people find hard to recover from.

But really, it goes deeper than that. When we vow to love honour and cherish, we make an obligatory promise that we will love the person we are with, putting them first above all others. We vow to honour them as a person, and honour the boundaries of the relationship.

Infidelity brings honour to no-one.

There is no cherishing going on either, if one of the partners is sneaking around making plans to meet his secretary after work, instead of coming home. (and don't kid yourself, the flowers and gifts he brings home to his wife at this time are not acts of cherishing, they are acts of guilt).

Your needs, trust and commitment have not been honoured by your partner, if he or she has allowed a third person to absorb attention and intimacy that should have been kept within the relationship.

Anyone who has lived through this type of betrayal will agree that discovery of an affair unleashes a torrent of emotions that are incredibly hard to digest.

Recovery takes time, as you ricochet wildly through a manic range of emotions, feeling sane and stable the one minute, to losing it completely the next.

The most critical thing to remember at this point is to allow yourself the time to absorb the enormity of it all. When emotions are on a helter-skelter ride, it is difficult to understand anything, or to make any constructive plans or take decisive action.

Although your first impulse may be to pack your bags, take the kids out of school and move to the other side of the planet, it might not be the best thing for all concerned.

Stand back from the situation and look at it from as many different angles as you can to gain a clearer perspective. Before you even ask whether you want to save the marriage or have the offending partner shot at dawn, take time to recognise and honour what you are feeling.

The stages of healing

The emotional fall out once an affair has been admitted is immense, and most people will ricochet between the first four stages of denial, anger, bargaining and depression repeatedly, in rapid succession, (and sometimes all at the same time). It is entirely normal to wake up in the morning and refuse to hear anything more about it, and just want to put it all behind you, only to get to the office and be seized by an insatiable craving for details of how it started, where they met, how long it had been going on, what they did together, why it lasted so long.

If can take up to two years or even longer to work through these stages, and to reach a level of acceptance.

Figure 11: The Road to Healing

Denial	**Responses ranging from:** It's not true. I don't want to know anything about it. It doesn't matter, we can recover from this, we'll just put it behind us and never speak of this again. I choose to believe what you are telling me, not what I now know to be true. *Or:* Becoming absorbed in an obsessive or physically intensive activity e.g.: getting blind drunk, or running a marathon to get it out of your mind, or deciding to remodel the kitchen and ripping out all the kitchen cabinets – anything really, as long as you have something else to focus on that can absorb all of your attention.
Anger	**Response:** Physical violent acts of attacking the other party, or the unfaithful partner, wrecking the home or his belongings, uncontrollable rage in inappropriate situations, self-destructive acts.
Bargaining	**Response:** Tell me what to do to fix it, tell me what did I do wrong? Needing a period of intense questioning, going over the issue again and again in an attempt to just understand why. (If I can just understand why this all happened, then I can put it behind me, if you make me understand what I need to do to fix it, then it will never happen again). *Also:* Trying to improve self-image, like dieting or making myself appear more attractive; if I look thinner, sexier, prettier, then you will want me more.

Depression	**Response:**
	I am not good enough, not worthy enough for you, you deserve more than me, of course you would prefer anyone else to me, what can I possibly offer you that would make you want to choose me? I don't blame you in the slightest for not wanting me anymore.
Acceptance	**Response:** It happened, It's done. There is nothing I can do to change the fact that it is done, but I can use the information I have learnt to move on from here. This is not the end of the road, but a part of the journey, and I have choices now – I can choose to stay with my spouse, or I can choose to end it. I will choose what honours my needs and boundaries, and will not allow myself to compromise the honour that I deserve to have for myself.
Healing	**Response:** As I begin to accept what is, as I begin to honour who I am and what I need, I allow myself to examine the relationship from a different perspective. Can it in this form give me what I need? Can it honour me? If we are both willing and able, can we change the relationship in the future to honour both of us. I look back on the journey over the past few years with this experience, and can see how much I have learnt and how to benefit my life with this new wisdom and understanding.

Can you recover from an affair?

It is possible to recover from an affair, and for the marriage to actually be strengthened as a result - not from the affair, but because the process of recovery for both partners unites them together in a common goal and journey.

It demands that both partners explore their innermost fears and doubts about themselves and each other, so that they can slowly begin to build bridges of trust and intimacy, belief and comfort again.

When Sam learnt of her husband's affair her first thought was how would they all survive without him? "I went into a complete spiral about whether I could manage with the children, whether I earned enough to raise them on my own, terrified that he would take all the furniture or insist I sold the home. I panicked about the very practical issues of who would drive my youngest son to sport practice each Wednesday, or how would we cope with the garden now, and I felt so very scared of dealing with it all on my own."

This an entirely normal response to finding out about an affair (how will I cope without you?), yet when there is no desire to resolve the real issues that prompted the affair in the first place, and we decide to stay together simply for the 'sake of the children', or because financially 'we cannot afford to leave each other', no healing can take place, and the marriage just limps along without any resolution for either partner.

When Greg came round a few months later to ask for a reconciliation, (the affair with his sister in law had burnt through its physical passion, and they had tired of each other rapidly when they had constant contact with each other), Sam took him back immediately. "It was such hard work being a single parent, shouldering all the responsibility for the household and trying to make ends meet. I was relieved when he came back."

Ultimately, the decision on whether to stay together rests on a few very simple, honest questions:

- Do we still love each other?

- Do we actually like each other? (It's possible to love someone without actually liking them, and vice versa. For a long term relationship to ever succeed, you need to not just love someone, you have to *like* who they are as well).

- Was the affair the result of a deeper malaise within the marriage that can be fixed?

- Do we want to try to repair this relationship? (if one person is unsure or unwilling, then nothing can be accomplished. It takes two committed intentions to recover after an affair, not just one).

- Am I willing to hear and see the other person's point of view, no matter how painful and uncomfortable it may be to acknowledge? Am I willing to explore my point of view and inner self?

- Are we both prepared to do whatever it takes, for however long it takes, to make this work?

- Am I staying only for the children? If the answer to that is yes:

  o What are they learning from this relationship that sets their emotional programme in place?

  o Am I simply suppressing my needs because I perceive that my children's needs are greater?

  o Can I still be a loving, effective, active, participatory parent, and treat my partner, their other parent with respect that is necessary in a relationship?

  o Would they be better off with two happy parents living apart, than with two unhappy, bitter parents living together?

A psychologist friend of mine once told me: *The kindest thing a parent can do for their child is to be kind first to the self.*

Which means that you have to be prepared to answer the question honestly: *What is in this instance that is the kindest thing that I can do for myself?*

It is vital that both parties realise that a great wounding has been done to their relationship and each other, and that it is the responsibility now of both to work towards it, not just the guilty party who had the affair. If you have decided to stay together and make it work, then both need to work at it.

The guilty party needs to accept that he or she will be subject to intense questioning, insecure behaviour, lack of trust, reassurance of affection and fidelity, for a long time to come. You cannot expect your partner to just sweep this up under the carpet and behave like it never happened. *It has happened,* and a lot of pain and scarring has resulted from this. Be gentle with your reassurance, sincere in your promise that you are committed to the relationship and to your partner, and that you are remorseful for the wounding that has been caused.

This requires constant attention, and constant reassurance. For how long? For as long as it takes.

The wounded party needs to accept that he or she was willing to try again, which indicates that he or she needs to be prepared to seek healing and a space of acceptance that will enable them to put the affair aside, and not keep dragging it into scrutiny again and again.

Recovery demands patience and compassion for the other party as well as toward the self, which means that continued punishment by going over old ground again and again does not help either of you.

There is no compassion for your partner if at every turn you point fingers of recrimination and blame; it delays their healing process.

There is no compassion for yourself, if you brood on it endlessly without seeking healing or counselling, it will delay your healing as well.

If you cannot put it down, and move beyond it, it is unlikely that you will be unable to save the relationship.

- Recognise this as an event. A hurtful, painful event it is true, but an event with a finite time and space attached to it.

- It is not all of your relationship. Before this occurred, you had a history and a connection, untouched by this pain. Focus on what was good and honourable before, and use that as your starting point for recovery, not the pain and fear of the infidelity.

- You had a previous point where you committed to each other. Re-examine what made you commit to each other then, and whether it still holds true.

- It is a good idea to reflect on what qualities keep you together even now, after the relationship has been wounded.

- Set common goals together, and put action plans in place to work toward them. A common effort unites and binds, and encourages a space where a rediscovery – or even a newer more real discovery of each other can take place.

If you decide an affair is OK

Kerry and her husband have reached an agreement in their marriage. They like each other and love their married relationship, but he travels extensively, and spends a lot of time in his company's office in France. "It has got so that he is away from home for two weeks at a time, every six weeks or so, " said Kerry. "It made sense for us to buy an apartment in Paris, to have a little car there, and to literally set up another household over there."

Her husband loves his work, thriving on the pressure and would hate to give it up. "I recognise how important it is to him, because he is truly doing work that he loves and I can see how much it stimulates him," she said.

When he told her about six months ago that he had spent the weekend with a woman from the Paris office, she was at first distressed and angry. "But the more I thought about, the less it worried me," she says. "I know he loves me, I know his first interest is me and the children … but he also has a life away from us as well. I didn't see her as a threat, rather as a part of his household, helping him to feel more secure and comfortable there."

Her friends and family think she has completely lost the plot, and that she should divorce him. "I love him," she says simply. "We have been living like this for years, and our marriage works. So, he has another woman that he is sleeping with every now and then. It doesn't affect my life, it happens in a different country, and I never have to confront it. At the end of the day, it simply didn't matter enough to affect our marriage."

When to walk away

> *You got to know when to hold them*
> *Know when to fold them*
> *Know when to walk away*
> *Know when to run ….*

Kenny Rodgers, The Gambler

Sadly sometimes, even after all the inner work on healing your own woundings, even after all the work on creating safe and mutually respectful relationship boundaries and after all the work on honouring your partner's needs, you just cannot disguise the ugly truth of the situation ... that it is not working for you, and no matter what you do, you cannot make it work, in a way that honours who you are.

And out of self-respect you reach a point of non-negotiable decision.

I deserve so much more than this.
I am worth more than this

Julie was so angry when she found out about Darren's lies and repeated betrayals that she wanted nothing more to do with him. It couldn't have happened at a worse time for her; she had quit her career in order to go back to university to study psychology, and so there was no money coming in. "I had to drop out of university to go back to work, and the kids and I moved into a pokey little house in a dingy little suburb, while he sold the family house and brought a huge house on the other side of town. While we were eating Weetabix for supper three nights a week, he was buying himself a new car, new clothes, and swanning off to parties and events with girls half his age hanging on his arm.

His mother told me to let him sow his wild oats, and he would be back within a year; we had gotten married so early, that he had never had chance to enjoy himself. I looked at the way this man was behaving, and knew that I detested him, and had done so for such a long time, and could never bear to have him touch me again.

The choice was simple. I would rather struggle financially than spend another day as this man's wife. He did come back as his mother had predicted, but by that time I proven to myself that we could survive. Not well, not luxuriously as we had before, but we could survive without him.

Key Points of this chapter

❖ Buy yourself time before you respond to what you think is going on, by breathing.

❖ Become conscious of breathing into that part of you that holds the unease and distress and allow your body response to come back to normal before you engage with your partner.

❖ Examine critically whether there really is something to worry about. Sometimes the triggers to an insecure attack are not grounded in any type of reality, but more in conjecture and fantasy.

❖ Sometimes, however where there is smoke there is fire, and affairs do happen. Infidelity dishonours everyone who is involved and is one of the worst betrayals within a relationship.

❖ It is possible to recover from an affair, but both partners need to be willing to allow the process of healing, and the time it takes will differ from couple to couple.

❖ There are really only a few reasons to stay together after an affair. The most critical of all are whether we love and like each other, and whether we are willing to find healing together.

❖ When, despite all your inner work, all your committed energy to the relationship, you cannot find any honour left to support you, sadly, it is time to walk away.

Self Reflection

1. How can I operate from within a space of power, and respond to what truly is happening and not react to how what I fear or imagine makes me feel?

2. Am I in the process of recovering from an affair or betrayal? Where am I on the scale of denial, anger, bargaining, depression, acceptance, healing?

3. Am I willing to see my partner's perspective, and to act with compassion for them and for myself in order to work toward healing together?

4. What common goals and objectives can we work towards together to unite us once more as a couple?

Chapter Twelve:

The search for self

Our behaviour today as adults, unless we have become aware of our patterns of thoughts and actions, will tend to be reactive, as opposed to proactive.

We live, work and play alongside each other, in a seemingly individual pursuit for wealth, health and happiness. Yet, from the moment we take our first breath we are led, guided, moulded and conditioned to adapt our behaviour to suit the environment, the situation and other people's expectations.

Of course this is necessary: humanity is a social construct, and operates through various communities to form societies, each with its own rules and mores of behaviour.

Through observing and mimicking others at work or play firstly within our families, then as we grow older in our smaller community of schools, churches and sports clubs, and later through larger societal microcosms like university or corporate work, we learn how to negotiate through life. We discover what is required in order to be successful in our career, in our finances, in our studies.

We learn how to have successful relationships with others, what behaviour is appropriate in the classroom or the boardroom, what strategies are certain to win us friendships (and approval) and what are guaranteed to isolate us from the crowd (and earn certain disapproval in the process).

The world tells us to have self-confidence, self-belief, self-trust, self-worth. The biggest irony of all, however, is that from the moment we take our first breath we are conditioned, not to be ourselves at all, but to be what others have shaped us to be. We behave and act, not from a sense of Self, but from the space of No Self that we have been trained to become in order to survive, - and hopefully become successful in society. We obey the rules, and the reward is acceptance, which makes us feel confident that we can play the game.

And all the time, we believe it is I, Me, Myself, who is doing all of the work.

Who Am I?

The answer to that question is complicated.

I am a product of my upbringing, of my conditioning, the beliefs I have formed because of this conditioning, the values and morals I have put in place as a result, and the behaviours and actions I do because of this upbringing

I am also a product of my past genetic inheritance, from my parents, grandparents, great parents and beyond, of their physical and emotional conditioning

And yet, and yet ... Isn't there more to me than this? Is who I am simply the joining of my past with the indeterminate effect of my future, or is there more?

That more is the Self.

Not the self that exists because of your ancestors conditioning and its effect on your physiology, emotional and mental body, nor the self that exists because it has been trained into this shape and moulded into this form, by the key players in your life.

The self that is unique and individual, beneath all the layers of what is appropriate, expected, rewarded or required.

To find the Self inside, we need to be prepared to question and explore and challenge how the world has shaped us, and how it sees us, and be prepared to see who we really are.

Beneath our actions and behaviours, beneath our values and morals, beneath our core beliefs and societal conditioning lies the potential for the most important relationship you will ever have: with yourself.

Only then can we begin to find and finally understand the meaning of Self Worth and Self Belief.

Finding the Self Within

It's not an easy journey: society discourages too much focus on the self; we are meant to form together in homogenous groupings and live external lives, not go inward on a solitary journey of singleness in a voyager of self-discovery.

We use words like self-obsessed, selfish, self-centred, self-rewarding, self-satisfied to convey our displeasure and discomfit at those who look for a deeper meaning to who they are. Society, you see, thrives not on the understanding of the self, but on the negating of the self for the greater good of the community or grouping, judging the roles we play, and bestowing upon us approval, recognition and acceptance if we play our roles right.

And the mistake that we all make is that we link the worth and the value of who we judge ourselves to be, with society's approval of the *role we play* and *what we do,* not on *who we are.*

Our self-worth and confidence and esteem is not centred on the self at all, but based so fragilely on our behaviour and actions. It is something that exists externally from who we are, something that needs to be earned and that can be taken away at a moment's notice.

If we always see ourselves through someone else's eyes, however, we only see the reflection of their opinion and understanding of what is real, - and, it must be remembered, through *their own layers upon layers of conditioning, core beliefs and filters, morals and value judgements* as to what is appropriate and correct, and perceived correctness of behaviour and actions.

The truth of the matter, of course, is that the self is not out there, and can never be seen clearly through another's eyes; the self lies within, and waits patiently to be discovered and seen truly, through your eyes.

Journey to the Centre

And so the journey toward the self begins.

It is a journey that requires patience, understanding, honesty and a willingness to explore who or what else I really am. By challenging age old patterns and behaviours, beliefs or filters, and examining whether they still resonate with us, we begin to painstakingly chip away until we discover the truth of who we are.

It begins gently at first, and all that is required is that you begin to observe and watch, becoming a witness to your life at times, instead of fully completely associated with it.

It may sound contrary to all the spiritual advice which is to be in the moment, and experience the moment – how on earth can you do that if you are witnessing and observing instead of being involved? And yet, in challenging who you truly are, in this journey toward the self, the first step is not to be, but to witness.

When we are experiencing the emotion, fully engaged, we are responding to our environment.

Which means that as long as I am always reacting to my environment, my situation, my thoughts, my partner, I am always going to be disempowered, I am always going to be at the mercy of someone else's behaviour, without even being aware of it.

When we step back and allow ourselves to become conscious of our actions and behaviours, when we are able to observe and witness without judgement, automatically a new kind of mindfulness begins where we can begin to assess whether the behaviour is positive and edifying for ourselves, our journey and for those in our space.

When Sandra stopped to witness her behaviour, and to stand at a distance, without judgement, she was able to observe how destructive her one night stands and relationships with married men really were in her life - but more importantly, she was able to understand the situations she created that led to them happening, and also the value judgements she had developed as a result of her core beliefs.

Witnessing our behaviour from a distance also allows us to witness how other people respond and validate us or disapprove and invalidate us. It shows us very effectively how our worth becomes wrapped up in what we do, and how we deliver - not in *who we are*.

The unspoken message is: I will approve of you and find you worthy if you do or behave in this fashion. It is however, a fragile worth and value – what happens when you no longer do or behave as before? Do you cease to have worth or value?

As we look at the roles we play, the things we do, we become able to assess the worth that is attributed to each action, that we mistakenly latch on to as self-worth and self-value.

The Value Within

Once we have stripped away the levels that cover who we are, we are then able to ask the question: Who am I? What beliefs resonate with me, not the programmed response of my childhood?

Beyond the roles that I play, beyond the conditioning and training, beyond my schooling and education, beyond the work that I do, who am I? What values do I hold to be true, not the value of my family or community or even my nation, what holds value in my life?

Beyond the relationship that I am in, beyond the feelings and emotions, both good and bad, who am I?

Identity Crisis

When I moved to Germany, I met many women who were suffering from exactly this phenomenon; women who had either met their German husbands in another country and now 'moved home' with him, (just as I had with Franz), or women whose partners were here on contract, or women themselves who were here working a contract in an overseas office for a while.

All of us were in various stages of struggling to settle down and re-establish our lives, but for Angie it seemed harder than most. In her 'old life' in Boston, she was a qualified physiotherapist, with a thriving practise, and was booked solidly throughout the year. She also ran a small spiritual centre, holding regular meditation evenings, which was well established.

She had two children of primary school age, both at different schools, and was well known with both communities. As she said one day: "I was under no illusion that things would be hard when we moved to Germany, not least of our challenges was learning to speak a whole new language in my 40's. My husband is German, and for him it was a home-coming, for the rest of us it was an uprooting of our life, our normal, our existence, but we did it for him."

In the beginning of course, moving to a new country is full of new and exciting endeavours – it's called the honeymoon phase for good reason. The new country takes on a rosy coloured hue, as we look at a life that is so different to what we are used to that there can be no comparison. "In those early days life was busy – finding a home, and furnishing it, getting children settled into new schools, learning how things worked in this new land." she said.

But as life began to settle down into its new routine, Angie began to cast around for who she was to be in this new country. "Each morning I would get up and send children off to school, my husband off to work in a flurry of activity, only to have the day stretch endlessly before me, before they came home. Housework can only be done so much, before all is clean and tidy, spick and span. Windows really don't need to be washed every week.

"Here I was in this new country, without any of my activities or behaviours that had been normal in my old life, which had validated me and gave me worth in the eyes of others. I felt invisible, no longer seen, as though my life were becoming smaller."

Angie had wrapped up her Self-Worth with the actions she did and the roles she played, not with who she was. If we are honest with ourselves, we all do it on a daily basis.

Activity: Angie ran a busy holistic physiotherapy practice, and a small spiritual and meditation centre

> Relative Worth: I was good at what I did, and people found value in working *with me, otherwise they would go elsewhere and not wait to see me, or study with me.*

> In Germany, no-one knew me, nor what I did, and I was at a loss of how to market myself to a German speaking audience, plus there were all sorts of obstacles to me obtaining my professional license to practice here.

Activity: I was a mother with children at schools

> **Relative Worth:** *I was often asked to help at school functions, and knew all the other mothers in each child's class. We bonded together through sports events, endless cricket matches, and pizza making days.*

> In Germany, I couldn't even speak to the teachers to find out how the kids were doing in their bridging lessons, let alone volunteer to help out on pizza days. I would go to all the meetings, and smile an awful lot, and try really hard, but despairingly aware that 95% of what was being said went completely over my head! And far from being involved with the other mothers and sitting and chatting at sports functions, I was avoided because of course I was hard work to have a conversation with

Activity: I was a friend with a social life

> **Relative Worth:** *I was liked and wanted and invited to share people's lives through friendships and dinners, barbecues and social gatherings.*

> In Germany, I tried really hard to make friends with fellow English speaking expats, and joined a club and got involved with various activities, but really struggled to make friends of a like nature, for a long time. I felt really lonely.

Activity: I was an English speaker in an English speaking country

> **Relative Worth:** *I could communicate and make myself understood, help, ask for help, support and be supported. I was heard, and my voice mattered.*

> In Germany, in the beginning I could barely make myself understood, and certainly was lost in the rush of words that came at me day by day. I battled on, trying to learn by myself with a home learning programme, but felt disempowered, invisible, unheard, and unable to communicate. My world was becoming very small, and I could feel my Self Worth eroding with each episode, each encounter with the school or a shop keeper or even in a community of likeminded people at the local Meditation centre.

What was really happening was simple: Angie had linked her sense of worth, her sense of value as a person with the value and approval and acceptance she got from others because of the behaviours and actions that she did.

Did this mean that she was different, less than, because her behaviours had changed so drastically? Of course not. Did it mean that she felt less than, unwanted, invisible and unseen? Absolutely.

Angie said, "I felt invalidated on every level that previously had reinforced me."

Feeling desperately insecure as she tried to navigate this new, seemingly harsh terrain, she turned to her husband to restore her sense of Self. "He was unable to help though; all those roles that I had been playing had been external largely to our relationship. I was the same as I always had been to him; wife, lover, friend, companion," she said.

"I couldn't restore my sense of worth from him in all these other areas in my life, this was obvious. Not from any fault or lack on his part, but because I was looking for the reassurance and affirmations that the roles that I had played previously had supplied – and that was outside of his 'job description'."

"My behaviours and actions that had been the comforting norm of my daily life had been stripped away from me in one harsh rip. I had a choice now. I could either wallow in this space of nothingness, depression, loss of identity, ... or I could use this as an opportunity to witness and discover and explore, and find the core of who I really am, not the person *others* think I am because of the actions that I do, or even the person that *I* think I am because of the way people respond to me, but the depths and truth of who I really am.

Angie began to explore this feeling of invisibility, unwanted, invalidated, less than. When else in her life had she felt this way, so out of control, so worthless?

And as she began to contemplate on the episodes of her life, feelings of past events came to the fore:

- Feeling insignificant and worthless next to my husband's competent colleagues who were all qualified medical professionals like I was, but unlike me, they were able to express themselves fluently.

- Enrolling at university as a mature student, to study physiology and further my nursing diploma into a physiotherapy degree. "There I was surrounded by young exuberant, smart kids, feeling out of my depth before even walking into the lecture hall. Some looked at me and assumed I was the lecturer; when I turned up for exams I was mistaken for an invigilator. I was too old to fit into this group of youthful excitement and rapidly became unseen. What had I been thinking? Surely I was too old to learn and would have been far more appropriate in a knitting class?"

- The woman who watched as her ex-husband flirted with all women, young and old, into eating out of his hands with his charm and boyish good looks, who felt not good enough, not pretty enough, to hold his interest.

- An old boyfriend who compared the way she looked as a young woman looked to a vibrant vivacious (skinny) girl in their group of friends. "I have always been rather healthily covered, and had thought he found it attractive. I remember feeling cut to shreds and 'less than' next to her, and next to many other girls after that. I have been paranoid about my figure and weight ever since then, wow; I never linked my weight fetish to that experience!"

- The teenager who hangs in the shadows, with her face in a book, always on the fringe, because she thought she looked funny and strange because of her eyes, to the point that sometimes even the teachers didn't know her name. "I refused to go to my school reunion 15 years later; because I was convinced no-one would even remember that I was in the same classroom as them," she said.

- The young girl who watched her father 'choose' her sister when the family split up, and felt unworthy, discarded, less than, as they drove away and out of her life forever.

- A child on the playground, wearing a big patch over one eye, and glasses with bottle top lenses, unable to see very much at all, who couldn't participate in the games the other kids were playing. She longed to be part of the group, and to play with them, but was a liability on any team because she simply couldn't see. She felt useless, unable to contribute, eventually unseen.

- An old memory long discarded came up out of the blue, where, ever the silent child she sat, listening to her mother discussing her own broken marriage with a friend. "Of course, we knew the marriage was in trouble long before it broke down. It was the reason we had Angie, to cement the marriage back together."

- And the long nurtured belief that comment had spawned: "I had been conceived intentionally, to save a marriage, and had failed miserably at that task. I was simply not enough."

Not Enough

And of course, in a nutshell, this is crux of any jealous tantrum, any deep and abiding feeling of insecurity.

Not Enough. It's the silent scream behind every argument, behind the destructive behaviours and actions, behind the judgemental stance of our filters and beliefs.

Not Enough, not enough, not enough, echoes through our heads like a demonic mantra, until we end up believing its false promise and judge ourselves as non-worthy, and pull back from the relationship, the joy, the life, the experience.

And it is at this point that the most vital work must be done; only then can we start to break down this most basic belief formed at the very core of who we are.

It requires that we ask searingly penetrating questions and reflect on the answers, and the most clarifying way of doing this is to look at the issue from all perspectives.

When we find ourselves feeling deep within 'I don't feel that I am Enough. I am less than, not good enough, not worthy, not capable', it is time to stop and ask very simply:

> Not Enough. For whom? Who exactly do you feel not good enough for?

> Not Enough. For what?

> Not Enough. Says who?

> Not Enough. To accomplish what exactly?

And when the answer comes, follow it and explore what is coming up from within you.

For Example: I feel that I am _not enough_ for my husband who needs to flirt with all other women because I cannot give him what he wants.

Figure 12: Exploring Not Enough

What does he want?	Recognition, adoration, visibility from everyone he encounters, male and female.
Do you give him visibility and recognition?	Yes, all the time, but it is never enough. He always needs more, and seems to thrive on the attention of anyone else in the environment. My all just never seems to be enough.
What core belief is happening? When you give and give and feel that it is not enough?	That what I can give is never enough. If I was good enough, he would not need adoration from everyone, anyone else.
What actions and behaviours come from this core belief?	That I need to give more and more to try to satisfy him. And then I get angry and sarcastic and quite vicious because I feel like nothing I do is seen or holds any worth or value to him.
What happens when you withhold attention or get angry with him?	He seems to escalate his behaviour until he has 'all eyes on him'. And so I just withdraw and shut down completely.
What do you think his core belief is saying during the time?	I have never thought about his beliefs as being involved here ... Now that I think about it, I guess it would be something like 'If I am seen by others then I know that I exist, or am important in some way.'
What actions come from this core belief?	Be larger than life, be flirty and fun, be charming to everyone, because as they respond to you it confirms and validate that you actually exist.

What could you do more to fill this need?	His behaviour comes from a far deeper need for validation and to be seen as worthy, in everyone's eyes, not just mine. One person's approval is not enough for long ... he needs to be recognised by the group energy.
So, in what way are you not enough?	No one person could ever be enough to convince him that he is always worthy and valid, it's a self-worth issue inside of him as well.
And so understanding that he has a core need of not enough, how does this change your belief about your value of not enough?	It is my issue because it triggers a primal response of not enough within me. But it is also his, because he has a deep inner insecurity and fear of invisibility, which is why he behaves as he does.
How will this change your actions?	I can only take control of my own response, my own fear of not being enough, not his. However, I can act with compassion when he escalates his behaviour to become frenetically charming, to realise that he does so out of his fear of invisibility; at those times I can try to validate him, not ignore, withdraw or shut down.

When we followed this exercise with Angie's situation, she found herself deeply resonating with the phrase: *Not Enough. Says Who?*

> Not Enough to save the marriage - says my mother

> Not Enough to be asked to play with the other kids - say the kids on the playground

> Not Enough to satisfy the image of the sexy young girlfriend - says the image conscious old boyfriend

Not my voice at all, but the voices of other people throughout her life, who had responded from their own level of conditioning, through their own filters and belief systems, not to what they truly see, but to what they perceive to be true.

How can a tiny baby possibly save a marriage? What skills or knowledge or even possible actions can an infant perform that can save a marriage already in trouble? The answer is simple: It is not within her control to do so. The expectation for the parents, was that by bringing a new baby into the world together that they could regain some of that old intimacy and love that seemed to have left them.

Is the voice then simply an acknowledgement of failure between two people then, and not an inditement of intrinsic worth? Perhaps.

The point of course is that it is irrelevant what was meant at the time, or whether it was actually said in a way to indicate the blame for the broken marriage lay in the hands of an infant child. What is relevant is that the core belief that sprung into being at the point … Not Enough, Not Enough … which became reinforced and echoed through other people's voices over the years… until a young woman finds herself in an unfamiliar and seemingly hostile territory in a new country where she cannot communicate at the most basic level, and the response comes back…

Not Enough, Not Enough for what? "To learn German, to slot into a new way of life, to engage with the teachers, to make new friends, to start up my business again."

This voice that says Not Enough within you, whose voice is it?

> *It belongs to different people at different times in my life. It's not my voice after all. I have simply regurgitated the echo for such a long time that I believe it to be my voice.*

What coping strategy did you put in place as a result of these voices?

> *I pull away and withdraw from the situation, removing myself from the possibility of rejection.*

In the here and now, what actions are you implementing as a direct result of this coping strategy?

> *To withdraw away from any encounter where I have to speak German, to look for approval and validation within my husband's and children's eyes, to allow my world to shrink until it revolves around the household and garden.*

How do these actions serve you?

> *They protect me in the short term, by keeping me safe from exposing myself. In the longer term, they isolate me which will keep me imprisoned for far longer, delaying my integration into this new society.*

And understanding that these actions are counterproductive and not self-serving at all, what actions can you put into place?

> *I can take back the control and become proactive about planning a strategy to adapt to my new home.*

I am pleased to report that she no longer feels so out of control. "I recognised that my old behaviours and normal were no longer appropriate or valid for me in this new life," she said. "In order to make this life successful I needed to change the behaviour, which meant examining value judgements, filters, core beliefs, and deep insecurities along the way."

"I signed up at school to learn German, and struggled through the course, proving to myself that 40 odd is not too old after all to learn a new language. I made it a goal to speak to somebody every day in German, and surprise, surprise, new friendships began to spring up as people would respond to me and teach me new words or phrases. I volunteered for anything that needed doing at the kids schools, and tried really hard to speak to the other moms, and found that they were more than willing to help me.

"These days, they actually send their kids around to our house to get some English exposure!"

Unable to find a group of likeminded people to meditate and interact with, she started her own small gathering, and soon found friends amongst many different nationalities – German, Czech, British, Swedish, American, Canadian, and Chinese.

The actions needed to change, but in order for the actions to change that had to be a core realisation that although the relative value of the work and roles she had played in Boston had been taken away, the value of **who she was** remained unchanged.

Self Discovery

For each of us, as we explore each level of our journey, we are able to recognise the wisdoms that work, and those that no longer serve us.

Figure 13: The Journey to Self Discovery

Stage	Response
Actions and Behaviours	As I allow myself to become conscious of my actions and behaviours I can reflect on those behaviours that are positive and empowering for me and those around me, as well as those actions and behaviours that I repeatedly do that have negative consequences to me and my environment, in terms of Work actions Relationships Finances Spiritual Sport and Health Home Self-development (study and growth) The people in my space approve and validate me by the following actions: _______. The people in my space disapprove and invalidate me by the following actions: _______. The worth and value that I believe I have because of the actions I have: _______.
Value Judgements and Filters	I recognise that my behaviours and actions are really the result of my value judgements and filters that have been put in place over the years, in the various areas of my life. As I speak these value judgements out verbally, I will allow myself to ask whether these are really

	my values and judgements, or whether I have borrowed them from a powerful figure in my conditioning phase? If I close my eyes, and speak my value judgement silently in my mind, whose voice is used to express this judgement? Do they add value in my life, or is it time to challenge and question their appropriateness right now?
Core beliefs	I recognise that my core beliefs are the direct result of my conditioning, both primary and secondary, and that they have been reinforced through experiences over the years. If I am honest with myself, my core belief about what is required in order to sustain a successful relationship, is ________. Is this mine, or have I absorbed this core belief along with my conditioning over the years? Does it add or remove value from the relationship?
Conditioning	The loudest voice in my primary conditioning years (generally 0–5) was ________. The strongest messages were ________. In my secondary conditioning, (generally 5–13) the strongest memories of my sense of developing self are ________. The strongest feelings from this time period are ________. In my reinforcing years of high school and university, I learnt that I had to do ________ in order to achieve validation and acceptance from the group. I adapted and fit in by doing ________. Or I switched to a different group where I was accepted more easily because I ________.

> The worth and value I have due to my upbringing and conditioning ________.

When you work through this exercise with honesty and from a space of witnessing truly what is, instead of being fully absorbed in the moment, we start to realise that when our worth and value largely comes from other people around us; or as a result of actions and behaviour; or due to possibly out-dated filters and core beliefs; or has been instilled in us as a behavioural measure throughout our conditioning phases.

More importantly, you begin to realise that it is:

a) **Conditional**; it is dependent on others opinions and views of us. When we 'perform' consistently with their positive expectations we receive approval and therefore value. When we fail to 'perform' that value is taken away or withheld.

b) **Transitory**; dependent upon a time frame (the period for which I have approval), and not upon the intrinsic inner nature of who I am.

c) **Penetrating**; it matters not whether it is real or true. The impact of our actions is returned to us by others responses, and we absorb the messages of worth versus non worth at the earliest possible age.

Self-Worth becomes a Choice

In 2003 I started my studies in Neuro-Linguistic Programming with South African expert, Jimmy Kyriacou. He used to tell this story to illustrate the intrinsic value of worth that we all hold, whether we are aware of it or not.

Imagine, he said, that you are walking through the most beautiful garden, when you hear the sound of children laughing and giggling. It's an irresistible sound of unexpressed joy and happiness, and you are drawn to observe and watch as toddlers run around, exploring, experiencing, absorbed in the world around them with delight. Everything is wonderful; the butterflies, the dancing sunbeams through the trees, the leaves blowing in a sudden flurry as a breeze blows through the playground.

You realise as you look at these children, that they represent pure potential. Their future stretches away before them, and as they are now, they can be anything, become anyone, achieve everything that they set their mind to.

Imagine, he said, that you are then given a clipboard and a pen, and you have to walk through this irrepressible bunch of giggling tots, and you have to decide which children are worth it, i.e. those that deserve to have a good life with happy experiences and a contented adulthood, and those who are not worth it, those who deserve to be scarred and hurt and humiliated by life's experiences.

What would you do?

It cannot be done, can it? Because each shining little face, each grubby pair of hands, each enquiring little mind with its constant 'why, why, why', deserves to be happy, deserves to have a good life, deserves contentment. Why? Because they are all worth it.

Imagine, he then said, that as you are walking through the group of children, that you spy one who looks just like you did at that age, playing happily, completely absorbed with the task at hand, feeling safe and secure in their worth.

As you get closer, you realise that it is you - and you stop to watch for a while remembering the simple joy of just being.

And then imagine, he said, that you could sit down next to this little tot, this shining, glorious, hopeful expression of *pure worth*, and holding tight to this younger you, you made a promise that you would never let them forget how valuable, how worthwhile, how beautiful, how *good enough*, more than good enough they are. And that you would always honour this moment of joy, of happiness, of wonder at just being.

And breathe that realisation into you. That within you, at the very core of you, beneath all the conditioning and negative beliefs that spring from it all, is this effervescent joy of knowing that in this moment I am Good Enough.

I have always been so. I just forgot it for a while, is all.

Self-Worth, when it is all said and done cannot be given to you. It cannot come from the eyes of others; it cannot be as a result of our achievements - all of that after all is transitory, and conditional, not a permanent value that we can trust implicitly.

Self-Worth is only to be found within, and, having realised who holds it, making a choice to honour it, realise it and value it.

And in the process realising: I am Good Enough. For Me!

I am Good Enough. Says who? Says Me!

Key points for this chapter

❖ Society forces us to behave in ways that often negate the self for the greater good of the larger family or community group

❖ Our concept of self or non self is formed at the earliest age and self-discovery is frowned upon as selfish and self-centred

❖ We are products of our genetic blue print just as surely as we are shaped by our emotional blue print

❖ When we measure our worth through the eyes of others, we must remember that they see us and respond to us through their own filter and judgments, and not as we truly are.

❖ The journey towards the self means that we have to examine the roles that we play, the actions and behaviours that have come into being as a result of core beliefs and value judgements

❖ This can be an uncomfortable journey, and precipitate an Identity Crisis of sorts, as we try to discover who we truly are

❖ Self-worth is not out there. It is an inner quality, and it is, once all is said and done, a choice

Self Reflection

1. Who am I really? Behind the actions and behaviours, behind the values and beliefs, behind the conditioning, who am I really?

2. What actions and roles do I support that create a false sense of temporary value and conditional approval in the eyes of the others.

3. What actions no longer serve the emerging sense of self and need to be discarded or adapted?

4. When I stop to witness my behaviour and what I do, do I see the value of who I am, or do my actions obscure that inner value?

5. When I follow the voices within that say not good enough, whose voices are they?

Chapter Thirteen:

Claim the Pedestal

Is that all it takes? I hear you ask. Is that it, all I have to do? Fix all of that and I will be free of this jealousy and crippling insecurity forever?

There is one last step, and just as crucial as the ones before it, and then yes, you will be free.

You have to **CLAIM YOUR RIGHT TO STAND ON THE PEDESTAL**

When we suffer under the weight of jealousy, it is because we feel that someone else … hell, everyone else … has the right to stand on the pedestal. Anyone *but me!*

In our last overwhelming argument about his ex I screamed at my husband that I was so sick and tired of *her* standing on a pedestal that I wanted to be mine.

"I want you to put me up on that pedestal, I want you to elevate me to that point, I want it to be me standing up there," I yelled at him.

I will never forget how he came and knelt in front of me, and held my face in his hands.

"Honey, you need to put *you* up on that pedestal", he said. "I can't do it for you. You have to believe that you deserve it, that it's yours, that's it waiting for you."

"I've tried so hard to put you up there, but you won't let me. Now I am begging you to see that the pedestal is empty. It has always been empty, that's why I never married her. I didn't love her enough to make her my wife. I didn't want her to be anything more than a temporary girlfriend. If I had, I would have married her, you need to understand that. I married you, and the pedestal belongs to you, and you need to claim your right to stand there."

He was right. I was waiting for him to see me as worthy enough, for him to place me there, all the while not realising that unless I claimed my right, and saw myself as worthy, I would never be able to stand up straight on any pedestal.

"I finished my relationship with her years ago," he said gently. "It is time that you allow yourself to finish your relationship with her too."

Through my own insecurity and jealousy I had forged a relationship with his ex, based on my own filters and misconceptions, based on my own inadequacies and doubts. It was a relationship where, even though I had never met her, never even spoken to her verbally, she held all the power, *because I had given it to her.*

I had placed his ex on the pedestal, and until I took the power away from her, she couldn't get off it.

It meant that it was time to take my power back. In the process, it meant that I had to give myself permission to end *my* relationship with her.

Healing the self means far more than healing the emotions, the thoughts, the relationships, the situation, the past, our thoughts about the future.

It means empowering the truth of who you truly are, every single facet of who you are, to stand up straight and strong and secure in your absolute knowledge, until every cell in your body, whispers, says out loud, SHOUTS with the power of your intrinsic worth and right to be happy and existent and loved.

And to finally, to:

> *Claim your right to stand on the pedestal of your life.*

Did I heal from this, is what you want to know now. Did this help? Did I resolve it once and for all?

> *Yes.*

How did it change who I am?

> *I lost weight, shedding effortlessly the extra kilograms that I had stored up over the years. I had carried her weight as well as mine for far too long, and she was heavy. When I finally put her down, I lost weight.*
>
> *I no longer looked at myself obsessively, comparing myself to other more beautiful women. I no longer anguished about every new line or wrinkle on my face.*
>
> *I relaxed, so much so that my kids, and my family commented on the difference in me.*
>
> *My business in Munich took off with a bang and I made friends, true, real friends not just occasional acquaintances.*

And my relationship with my husband?

> *It's beautiful.*
>
> *We haven't argued about her since. Finally it is done, and finished and it is well and truly over. Our relationship has escalated to a whole new level, and it's because I feel confident and secure that he is with me because he loves me.*
>
> *I trust him. More importantly, I trust my SELF. Finally, I gave myself permission to stand up straight on the pedestal of my life.*

Chapter Fourteen:

The Gold Within

I started this book with a story; my story. It is appropriate to end with a story that belongs to everyone.

It is the story of The Golden Buddha, and is set many years ago, in a rural village in eastern China.

Like other villages scattered through the countryside, it survived off what it's inhabitants could farm from the land and their closely tended herds of goats and sheep. Life happened here in the slow, steady pace of the seasons as it had done for centuries.

It was an unremarkable little village in every way, except for one. A narrow, winding path led steeply down the mountainside to a hidden grotto where a water fall cascaded down sheer cliffs into a pool of crystal clear water.

And there, almost hidden by the trees and the shadows of the grotto, was a statue of Buddha. Nine foot tall, it was covered in gold which shimmered in the afternoon sunshine, as the haze from the waterfall formed a rainbow that danced over his feet.

It was renowned as a sanctuary of peace and clarity. Indeed, it was said that any who meditated at the foot of the Golden Buddha would receive insight as to who they truly were in this life, and what their life purpose was, and so many travellers came in pilgrimage to come and sit in contemplation and inner reflection at the foot of this magnificent statue.

It had been so for centuries.

Until one day, a priest brought news of an invading army, with guns and canons, who were destroying the temples of the land as they overpowered their people.

Powerless to fight back, their weapons of wood and steel useless against guns and dynamite, the people of the land had no choice but to stand by helpless as their homes, their way of life, their traditions and their faith were ransacked and pillaged by an army that had no understanding that they were desecrating far more than just a way of life.

"They will destroy our Golden Buddha", said the Elders. "We must find a way to protect it."

The village elders met that evening, talking late into the night but the task seemed impossible. The Buddha was too heavy to move. What could they possibly do to hide it away so the invading army didn't destroy it?

It was a young man who came up with the solution. He suggested that they covered the Buddha with clay from the bottom of the pool, and obscure the gold and the shape so that anyone looking at it would just see a piece of rock.

It was, agreed the elders, a most ingenious plan, and so the villagers worked hard to cover their Buddha. Their task was soon accomplished and the clay left to bake and set in the sun, until anyone looking at it would never be able to tell that it had ever been a Buddha before.

The hungry army came through the village devouring crops and meat, decimating their winter stores, and herds of sheep and goats. And finding nothing else of value, it soon moved on, attacking and subduing and controlling the land.

Years passed, and the land remained occupied. No-one dared to repair the temples and they fell into decay, crumbling beneath the trees and foliage that were their only worshippers now. Religious expression was forbidden, punishable by death.

The elders of the village all died, and people stopped talking about their hidden Buddha. The young man who had come up with the plan over 70 years before, grew old and confused, and could no longer remember whether the Buddha had been real or whether it was a story he had heard about as a child. There were so many fables of hidden treasures in this land after all.

Until one day, a young man came to the village; he had set out many months before with a desire to explore the land, to discover what lay beyond the mountains that had been his home all of his life. He had walked for many miles, and his feet were tired, his legs worn out. Upon hearing about the beautiful grotto, he set off slowly down the narrow, winding mountain path exclaiming in delight as he reached the bottom of the natural wonder and beauty of this hidden place. He swam in the sparkling water, feeling its cool water refreshing his energy after the heat of the day.

After a time he waded out of the pool and still wet, settled himself against a strange looking outcrop of rock, resting quietly with his eyes closed, feeling languid in the afternoon sun. He was startled out of his peaceful contemplation when something hard hit him on the head, following by a scurry of stones and dust from the rock he had been leaning against. Curious he stood up to see what had caused the disturbance – a monkey perhaps, or a bird?

As he examined the rock above him, he thought he could see something glinting dully in the sunlight. Was that something buried underneath the rock and stone?

Carefully he began to chip away at the rock, exposing more and more of this strange metal. It had no shape, no feature, and he was bemused as to what it could possibly be.

Standing back to gain a better perspective, he suddenly realised what he had uncovered. It was the shape of a forearm, as it flows towards the wrist, and he grew excited as he realised that the rock was covering an enormous golden statue.

 Excitedly now, yet with infinite care and patience, he worked, exposing the statue from its prison of clay and stone. Day after day he worked, gently removing the covering of clay and mud the villagers had placed over their most precious Buddha almost a century before, to protect it and keep it safe.

Slowly, painstakingly, the glory of the Golden Buddha emerged, seeming to glow in the light of the sun as the spray from the waterfall danced with breath-taking rainbows of colour around his feet.

In awe the young man knelt before this statue, realising that this was the forgotten statue, long since relegated to the realm of myth and make-believe.

In a blinding flash of clarity, he realised the true message of the Golden Buddha: That by following in the footsteps of the Buddha, people would begin to find their Buddha nature, their true selves. He realised that within each person was the potential of pure gold.

The inner nature of the man would reflect outwardly for all to see.

And he realised that the purpose of life was simple, when all was said and done. It was to honour the gold within every person he came into contact with, whether they were aware of their inner beauty or not. Because the clay and the stone that covered them, was just that - a covering and not the real person after all.

The moral of the story?

That when we enter into this life, we are Golden. The sunlight dances on us and glints off our skin. Rainbows shimmer around our feet. The possibilities that lay before us at the moment of our first breath are boundless and awesome to consider.

In order to protect us and keep us safe, *our Golden Self becomes covered with the clay and mud of our primary and secondary conditioning.* Sometimes this sets hard, and our journey becomes cast in stone, and we behave, think and feel as we have been trained to do, imprisoned in a mould not of our own making.

As time goes by, we forget who we truly are, and dismiss stories of regaining the power of our true self as myths, fairy tales, nothing really but a childhood story that bears little resemblance to the reality of life.

In order to rediscover the Gold within us, we have to be prepared to go on a journey, sometimes with no clear goal in sight, except for the desire to discover, learn, explore the world around and within us.

The impetus to act often comes from a point of pain or discomfit. Like the young man in the story, until a stone fell on his head and hurt him, he was a) quite content to lie in peaceful contemplation at the foot of the rocky outcrop and b) completely unaware that it was anything other than what he had supposed it to be: a funny looking rock at the bottom of the gorge.

Uncovering who we truly are demands hard work. It is not easy to chip away at years of conditioning and the moulding of years. It has been set in place by years of exposure to the elements of our life, as surely as if it had been exposed to the sun, wind and rain of forgotten decades. And yet, every now and then, if we stand back and look at it all from a different perspective, there is the hint of something glinting dully beneath the clay and conditioning of the years before.

It is a solitary work. The only person who can decide when and how to take the journey is yourself. You cannot decide for another, or force them to a place of perspective if they are not ready to, any more than they can decide for you – all you can do is work on yourself, by yourself, learning and assimilating your own insights and wisdoms along the way.

The answers are not 'out there'. The answer is within. The Gold does not lie in wealth, fame, power, control. Nor does it lie in other's beliefs and perceptions, nor what we see reflected in the eyes of others. The Gold lies within us, and once realised, the coverings and illusions of years of pain and hurt fall away, revealing the glory of who we truly are.

Accompanying CD

All the visualisations and actions in this book have now been compiled onto a Visualisation CD of the same name. Please go online to www.thesoullighthouse.com to find out more details about the contents, and also to find stockists near you.

References

All of the diagrams and theories have been personally developed by Susan Schöning, with the exception of Figure 4 in Chapter 5, which is based on the work by Eric Erikson's Stages of Development.

I have of course been influenced by certain works and theories as I have written this work.

* Practitioners of Ayurveda will no doubt recognise the link between Figure 2 in Chapter 3 and the Kapha, Pitta, Vata Doshas. For more information on Ayurveda and how it can affect the emotional, mental, body balance, please have a look at www.mapi.com, the official website of Maharishi Ayurveda.

* Harville Hendrix and Helen Hunt have also used Erikson's model of the Stages of Development, (Chapter 4). If you have found benefit out of this book, then consider also buying their series on Imago love, (Getting the love you want, Keeping the love you find, etc.). They are such a powerful series of books that I actually give them away to people as wedding or anniversary presents. For more information, have a look at their official website: www.harvillehendrix.com

* As a certified NLP Master Practitioner, I have of course used NLP techniques throughout this book. Many organisations and reputable teachers are available throughout the world. Browse on the internet to find an organisation near you.

* The work of Byron Katie is very powerful: *Loving what Is*. I have touched on this so very briefly, by asking her first few questions in *The Work*: "Is it True? Is it Really True?" The other questions are of course: "How do I behave when I believe this to be true?", and "Where would I be without this thought?" (Chapter 8)

* For more information on Byron Katie, please go to www.byronkatie.com, or www.thework.com

About Erik Erikson

Erik Erikson was a pioneering German psychoanalyst (1902 – 1994) who, in this behaviour model of The Stages of Development, explored the three aspects of identity, namely: the *ego identity* (self), *personal identity* (those personal characteristics and behaviours that make us who we are), and the *social/cultural identity* (the roles we play within our friendships, societies and communities).

This psycho-social theory of development explores the impact that external factors such as environmental factors (like parental care and involvement, community and society strictures and expectations, and so on), have on the personality and internal security development of the child on his journey from childhood to adulthood. According to Erikson, all of us pass through eight interrelated stages during our entire life cycle.

In the work we have covered, we have only gone as far as stage 6, ending at the stage of the *Young Adult* choosing whether he is able to be intimate with another or whether he chooses a life of isolation and pulling away from forming relationships.

There are two more stages according to this model, that of the *Middle Age Adult*, which lasts the span of our productive years (namely 25ish to retirement from active career life) and *Old Age Adult* - but, as they say in the classics, therein lies another story entirely!

Acknowledgements and Thanks

If I have learnt one thing over the past two years, it is that writing and publishing a book feels very much like having a baby. I thank God for those special souls along the way who through their presence, encouragement and sometimes damned stubborn refusal to let me give it all up and throw it away, have helped me to release this work.

- ❖ Mom, Joyce, Irene, Lana, Louise, Kirsten, April, Karl, Beryl, Roxey, Birgit, Amy. You have helped more than you can ever know and I am so very grateful for your enthusiasm, positivity and constant belief that this book contains a message that is important and which needs to brought out into the light.

- ❖ To all those wonderful people who shared their stories and pain with me, and gave me permission to use their stories, (as long as I changed their names). I have been there where you are, and I know how hard it is. I also know that now is the time to start toward healing, and thank you for allowing me to be part of your healing journey.

- ❖ Wisdom and learning often come to us through pain and ugliness. That is why the learning is so profound. I never thought that I would ever get to this point, but truly I am thankful for these experiences for being the catalysts for such profound healing in my life.

- ❖ To my children, who quite literally shut the door on me, and got stuck in on their own, with homework, housework and cooking, so that I could have the time and space to write. Thanks for the space guys, you are wonderful and I am grateful every day that you chose me to be your mom!

- ❖ To my beautiful, glorious husband, Franz. Thank you for seeing in me the beauty and the potential of who I really am, especially in those times when I couldn't see it myself. This book is largely due to your patience and because of the freedom you gave me to discover my own path to healing. Thank you for being my rock.

About the Author

Susan was born in England, but immigrated to South Africa with her family as a young child. She trained as a nurse after leaving school, but left to study journalism and public relations as she wanted to pursue a career in that field. After receiving her Diploma in Public Relations Sue worked for a number years gaining experience working for an industry newspaper and then managing the marketing department of an automotive company, before launching her own public relations and below-the-line marketing agency.

With her previous medical experience and knowledge, she began to adopt clients from the medical establishments, specializing eventually in woman's health issues.

Throughout all of this, Sue was an avid lay-student of comparative religion, spirituality and self-development, and her interest in this field took her on an intensely personal journey of healing and psychic discovery. She studied metaphysics and spiritual psychology for many years with an Indian Guru and spiritual teacher in Johannesburg, becoming more and more drawn to energy healing for self and others, within the mental, physical, body, emotional and spiritual bodies.

1999 she established her healing and counselling practice in Johannesburg, and over the years continued to expand her "counseling tool-box" to assist her rapidly growing client base, namely: Ayurveda - lifestyle, psychology and nutrition, Journey Therapy, Spiritual Counseling, Energy Healing, Metaphysics, Emotional Freedom Technique Practitioner, Imago Therapy, as well as a few of the more esoteric aspects of psychic development and healing. She also became certified as a Neuro Linguistic Programming Master Practitioner.

Over the years, she has become recognized as a public speaker, and is frequently asked to present at conferences and spiritual gatherings, women's health meetings, and other spiritual centers. She has appeared on radio and TV in South Africa many times, promoting her work.

Although she has written many articles, and training modules / booklets in her own capacity and hundreds of press releases and radio and TV reports as a PR agent, this is her first book.

It was inspired by two perspectives:

- ❖ Increasing numbers of clients, male and female, who were struggling to overcome jealousy and insecurity within their relationships, and who either "swept their feeling under the rug repeatedly" or actively destroyed an otherwise beautiful relationship. The more they explored the feeling of jealousy and insecurity in the relationship, the more they discovered it was seldom about the current event at all, but something far, far deeper that needed to be healed.

- ❖ Her own insecurity in her second marriage and feelings of inadequacy when comparing herself to her husband's previous girlfriend.

Sue recently moved to Germany with her husband and two teenage children. Her busy practice has adapted, and many of her clients made the "move" with her, switching to telephonic consultations and internet based workshops. She has also added clients from as far afield as the USA and Canada, United Kingdom, Peru, New Zealand, Dubai and India to her list, becoming truly international in her client base.

In 2010 she launched The Soul Lighthouse, and The Munich Academy of Metaphysics, both of which are growing rapidly in their new home.

For more information about her work, please visit www.thesoullighthouse.com